HOW I ESCAPED

MY ABUSERS

QUEEN WESTFIELD

DEDICATION:

I dedicate this book to my wife deodar Westfield and my (3) three son Farley Andrews Alvin Andrews and James farmer, for giving me the time and space to write my story in (2) books. part one, little girl grown to fast Hawaii avenue by queen Westfield a now book two how I escaped my abusers. she pushes me to achieve anything I want and wish to do. and these two books was a way to free myself from all my abusers that was still on my shoulders now because of her giving me the space and time. I am happy and free of all of them .my sons pushed me to do what I needed to do to get myself well and happy thank you my lovely wife deodar Westfield sons Farley Andrews Alvin Andrews James farmer.

ACKNOWLEDGEMENT

Everything I have written is the truth of all the things I have been through in my life and I am freeing my truths I am now able to acknowledgement that it was not my fault of the things I been through so I have forgiven everyone so I can be free I did it for myself not for then I can't be free if didn't forgive them first. I forgive all of you bless you on your journeys in life I forgive you.

INTRODUCTION:

I am queen Westfield survival of abusive relationships; I tell you how I survived them all in many ways by getting out by leaving and by writing these (2) two books letting my story to help other's in my same situation, I am 55 years old now. these (2) two books truly freed me from my abusers that's why I am a true survivor, I've walked away now I have written there them out my life off my shoulder's once you can do all three. you are a truesurvivier with in yourself so I hope my books help someone.

I don't see things like other people see then I need the logic from their way of coming up with their reason of why everything is a why, when, you ask real questions, that require real answers and you. get the lied from them of why did or didn't do something, they can't answer you because they don't see anything wrong. with their actions in the pain, rejection the neglect the inflicted on someone and no care in the world. she only knows how to take of my brother because he was a male she said it herself she only knew how to take care of him, and not me. so I got no attention from her do to that. fact he got a lot from her not me and no l not acting jealous I being honest I wore my own hammy downs from 6 grade to. high tile I was in the 9th grade then when I got my summer job I brought my self some clothes I didn't know how to shop for the different seasons because I brought all summer wear clothes for the 10th grade got now stuff for my first year high school I had new stuff I got from my summer job worked at the VA. hospital.

I got to walk around people like my mom but I didn't know it. they were like her and she was like them. being in this world and body, I some time fell like I am not myself. the main number one reason I can't go to sleep without meds is because I am an afraid I may never wake up as myself again it could be someone else controlling my body even though it looks like me and everything may seem that I am still there are so many my   head right now   trying to take over my mind I take meds   to make then stay away. and keep them hidden from the way I see them in the front of me. mirror a to once it is off I see those red eyes a crazy looking eyes. these monster are scary and mean to me the spirits are real and they are in plan faces I see then I can smell them sometimes is a scent I can't get rid of them. I don't eat crazy foods to make them come out. they just come. they just come when they feel like it. ever since I was a very young child I been having night terror since back as far as I can remember that's why I started sucking my fingers they were my security blanket. I can describe them all. I can tell you how tall or short they are, the scents of their perfumes or their colognes.one is a younger me yelling out for help from (mom)but she never is there for me. I keep all this stuff all to myself that people won't ever understand exactly what they have done .me sucking my fingers all my life is a calming-mechanism for me .it helps me calm my anxiety down on the scary feeling I feel inside from whatever is in there that would come out and we never knew it was a change because I would look that same almost act the same but whichever one of the person in me came out and look over. people don't believe that people have split personality. there are a lot of them walking the earth and never show or tell they on meds because society.

Says we're wired if we are like that on some crazy meds. That help us. but believe it or not mostly the ones saying all the negative talk. half the world is walking around here mad ,depressed, an smiling while all the time hiding their pain their feelings to cover their pain and bitch about our way of dealing with it just cause we took steps to do something about our healing don't knock us down ,we are already down trying to get back up on our own feet ,and once we do and meds is the way people have issues that others or should I say most people don't know about our want to know the be like you can get past all that all you need to do is this or you need to do that not worrying those words hurts because you still not caring about that person feeling or things they suffering from they not listening to the person in pain or suffering turn depression or patsies that's what I have . people don't know how we feel about what's going on in our head to try any explains to anyone or where this pain or hate rest comes from. why we don't see stuff like other people because there are not living though it so they don't and can't understand it and can't we got over it some people may have the same issues and are afraid to get help or even admit they even have one I have always felt different not knowing I was different from the rest of the kids around me I had. I had a hard time learning in school I was called lazy I wasn't lazy, I was I just didn't get it ,these pictures and reading never understood anything always carried around a headaches, but every one said I was faking it and now in my 30s I was.

Untold all my issues I have and had carried around all these years was real and I know from you had I. trough I learning school I told I can't and won't ever feel normal or get better when you talk about me healing from the stuff I am dealing with I can't be normal because I can't let this womb go it altered my life. it stopped my early on stages of potential by me not being able to learn like others and I can't let go because most of it is from my childhood trauma to my head that has caused me to have be lifelong issue that Dries can't fix at all at all. 4different top brain dry's said no they would not touch me they did not want to my life style now I would 99%be a vegetable. for the rest of my life and I would not know only thing around me or people I would be depending on someone 24/7 365 care strapped to a chair and bed. For the rest of my life not even knowing who will be taking care of me. without hurting me.so they recommend I take the meds for the rest of my life. I know I could not trust anyone to care for me let alone my children just my wife .and I have to keep the meds for the next 30plus years of my life. and I want my normal life with my wife for as long as I can a could give her my time I will be giving it my all to her and our children and our grandchildren. so I am on meds for pain level like thinking about all that a 2 or 3 anything above a 4 or 5 is can't move pain let me alone.

been put in the system no family would have taken them in as their own and I could not see them grow up I would have missed everything. just thinking about all that while seeing all these doctors about the pain in my head, bleeding nose with the supper electrifying migraine the real name for, that I have is called chronic cluster migraine's that never goes away. the level of pain in the only things that changes 1-10 hospital (1) easily 2-4 creeping up take meds every day. no matter the pain level to keep it at a level where I can focus and function. Anything over a 5 is bad means it will last for hrs. and maybe days spiking up to a (10) and that sets off my nose bleeds and my vertigo kicks in that's where the room is spinning around backwards and it moving at about 95mph and you don't have anything to catch you from falling this happiness. I need to be in the hospital getting my shots in my and in a iv an (2) two pills just to stop the vertigo and the nose bleeds, the one they do that they can give me meds for my headaches, it's a shot in the arm for an hour I have to sit in the hospital tile, they see I can do what they say before I can leave. and this is about (2) two to (3) three times a month the headaches are nonstop they came start while I am a sleep, they can wake me up out my sleep feel like I was hit in the head with an about that hard waking me up that.

I can't even wake up or movie have to wake my baby up and have her find my meds and get them for me before my nose bleeding starts or my vertigo kick in. you can't turn the lights can't move bed blanket or asking me about of questions my baby move really quick when I have one she get what I need and give it to me so I can move I get paralyzed .I can't move quick ,when I have a migraine it scary everyday cause I don't know how bad or long it's going to take   I could not escape from my dad I didn't get to escape from him tile he passed away .so that was my way out by my dad stealing away my innocents, he took away everything from me and made me a woman an my childhood was no longer mine I was a woman . before I was a child all this happened when my mom was or wasn't around can't say for sure, do to her Illness her mind was not present some time even though she was. I was burned with cigarettes just because I touched the pack. I know they fought a lot over me, because she left me alone a lot I don't remember her around much I saw both set of grandparents and my dad. I wanted to know all my life. What I couldn't have, I was there little (girl) nobody wanted. with a huge secret no, one knew about. I was not able to express or explain what was going on to me whom was I to tell. whom and what was I to tell I was with my dad the one that was hurting me I never knew it was wrong tile. was almost grown by this time have long gone. l know she disappeared from my life.

I then was shipped from the two houses of both grandparents .so confusion so lost just existing in the universe I knew and lived in. I was born with a target on my back is how I feel .and I don't know why am how it was put on me since birth. my parents killed me inside of me by their actions and leaving me to fend for myself after all the damage. they put on me through done to me by them and their friend of theirs. I couldn't and today still don't understand. most of them were her friend I can't recall any of my dad's friends being around except my god parents Denise and Larry.

No one else and Sherwood the 1st time I danced one time

for all then I was like 3-or 4 then. being at my grandparents home on Longfellow I learned over the years that they both only had a (6) six grade education, but that was because back then they needed to worth and help the family out my aunt (bay) bay lease, whom my grandma was named after raised her and got her a job in the school system. as a cook where she worked tile she could no longer cook or work retired at 65 and passed away at 72 in 2000, she would ask me how to do multiplication stuff so I wrote them on file cards for her. all the times table she needed it for measuring the food at work.

I taught her the way to measurements to cause I was in

cooking classes to in middle school. I know she couldn't read she always asked me to tell her what letters that came in the mail said she would hide them from my aunt rose and give them to me. to teach her. my grandparents worked at the era as an electrician he was there until he died he was 61 years old. he was my teddy bear he never knew that everywhere he would go in the car I would jump in the back seat I would lay in the backseat and look up at the sky as if I was in the ocean. headed to his sister's house aunt Frances or aunt Alameda house, I loved going with him because I could eat all the candy and soda I wanted everyone on my dad side spoiled me, I was the only grandchild, my aunts and uncle's news the truth about who Christina dad really was my grand pa's baby that's why no one was caring about her when he passed they were worried about me the most how was I doing in Losing my best friend and grand pa. I had lost my grandpa he was the other person that was nice to me like my grandma she was my play mate she played with me all the time. she let me make mud pies and dig in the front yard a lot she played dolls with me. all te time more than my dad he only did that bad thing to me. she would let me eat all the candy and chip.

I Wanted and Hawaiian punch drink soda, all weekend then I would play more and by dinner time I be.to full to eat my dinner she let me stay up late. with my aunt rose we didn't have a time for bed or being in the house we could stay out as late as we wanted to she was always throwing parties and doing these bus trip, trips that everybody in the block went with us we had a big bus like a grey hound come take us to the main parks like king's dominion, Hershey park, bush gardens, and ocean city. We got to do whatever we wanted down there. known as an adult as I had my kids I started learning that all the stuff they allowed us to do. Was wrong we always had boys over there. my grandparents would go to bed when company came over so we had the base-mental and upstairs living room area just not the third floor. I could make or get her male friends to do whatever I said like lotion my feet or my legs I was at the bar with my legs propped up and he did it. he would do it without me asking he was having a crush on me .and one day he came over to my house to hang out with me. we tried to be friends for while then he disappeared. Even though I wanted too. We became friends before he disappeared. we rode our bikes a lot to her boyfriend's houses. The guys met up with us in the park. Rock creek park .and hang out. I started smoking at 8 and I stopped at 18.i smoked my first joint at 13 at candy land park. that's the only time. we use to throw some wild parties in those days. I say wild cause it would 200only be coupled up people their close friend and ones that didn't have a mate couldn't stay I was dared to do what I did and I did it because I didn't want to go to be so I did it because I wasn't afraid of a dare I had to prove myself to all our friends. that I could back up my talk from all the shit talking I did on the phone .it was time for me to show I was as my mouth was so I showed up and showed out, I proved myself to, them all and after that day I was part of the group. After that I became ill rose, people didn't mess with me because they were afraid of her and they knew if I was like her I didn't play I was just, a little version of her and just as mean as her and was not afraid of any one and people knew not. to mess with me grownups people was afraid of because of whom my aunt was, so I could say a do as I please don't long fellow bust on my other grandma house I couldn't do any of that stuff so I was (2) two different people until I moved to Hawaii avenue then I didn't have to be no one but who I wanted to be myself at least I think and felt like myself. the person I had created to be me I don't know who or what I would or could have become if my life was any different life if my parents raised me themselves. How much different would it have been would I have finished school? would I have gone to college everything is a world could should? I? Now? I did it all in my own way, on my own time as my kids grew. everything educational wise I pushed

Myself achieve them. and my kids and my juicy pushed me to finish it since I, went for it. I had achieved my wanted it. I got a master's degree in culinary arts and science and baking pastry. Culinary arts. 4years of school with the help of my wife and my kids, I been out of school almost a year now and I miss it. I want to, cook so much more but I don't have the. Budget for all the dishes I want to cook I have learned so much in school all those years growing up on Hawaii avenue I didn't have food so that was the reason I wanted to cook so much food .so we my brother and I could have meals everyday .the little money she did give us I brought cookbooks but didn't or should I say understand how to read them so I was cooking stuff wrong or we still ate it .I started really doing cooking once I had my son's and then even more fancy food once I get in to culinary school there is so much to learn to cook out there . the way I saw as not having food growing up cause (mom) never cooked real food for us. my life dealing with health issues out of my control I have they came about I've had eight operations since 1998 2024. the first was in 98, and couldn't eat so 1 month I could only eat baby food. because my throat as so raw. being an orphan grown up alone its does something to you mentally and emotionally a mess. your children as adults they are traumatized for life, on all platforms of destructions, they can they can feel everything. the other way is to abuse their own, bodies. this part is a mess the up cycle of life because they may have watch their mom being abused in their life. and for the people that saw it and never said a word or called some help for us thanks. for all the sexual abuse i went through in the building we all lived in there felt like family. but turns out it wasn't family it was monster in human body forms, I wish someone would have stepped in and took over us didn't put ever family check on us whether they knew or not they never called us. unless they believe her stories of where we were. when she went up the house. let's just say from then till now I'm still am having some type of operation and we are now in the year2024 two operations on left breast twice in one in less than a year. that's wild I just thought about something the operations I just had were the same time done like the ones I had years ago April then Jan breast operation same thing both months my ones I just had Feb –march my nose and throat my hernia then200 feb-march again nose and throat and hernia, that was crazy. that what I go through operations twice for the same thing. the left side is bigger than the right side. these are things I went through alone my mom was not there .I was in DC an MD. things I can't stop from happening or control them the one person was all three of my son's they were my little protectors they were by my side everyday am took care of my breast when I came home he cleaned my womb up every day till it heal thanks .297you my son for that, Farley stood up to his step dad when he put his hands on me for the first time in 17years thank you my son for standing up as a real man that night. The time we move to NC I had to have another operation I had my hysterectomy and no help from my girlfriend my sons again helped me she could care less I was in pain. and they took my appendix out too. when I had my hernia fixed they took my gallbladder too. The things in. I had I'm throat were papilloma I had it twice and it will return again and again.

They will come back year after year can't say why just know they will. The ones in my throat there is no way to stop them. I am now on disability do to my childhood all story in my first book (little girl grown to fast Hawaii avenue by queen West Field) I am having more work done on my hands this time. if it not one thing it's something else. my sons have been my rocks for as day one for me to still be here today I am great full to have three amazing sons. they have bought me many moments of joy and pride in them. they are everything to me. I have gotten these digress in my field and now I can't use my last three .so I achieved my goals in getting them and I enjoyed getting them and I'm am proud that I did it my family is proud of me also. so I guess I did ok. I wear and wore many hats in my life and now I can rest them All. an I can sit back and pick. a choose.

Which hat I want to wear for any days now. I mostly just want not wear my chef hat in the house. an make great food. For my family. now that I have said that about myself how many friends do I really have I can count on one hand truly. family, work, activities busy schedules, yam we all have them. if I can find the time to send out a text, a call, a message, then if I'm your friend or family you should be able to do the, same. no pressure though, if they were there they would have known what I was going through right in front of them everyone turned a blind eye on me when I left Roxboro pl. it like they say out of sight out of mind so it's true .all those years don't know me you knew of me it's been years since we talked or hung out so I'm not that little girl from high school or the girl with three small boys my boys are 37 ,35, 31 ,that's how I know nobody knows me we been friends since elm, school and when was the last time we talked ,when was the first or last time you was at my apartment on Hawaii avenue. can you tell me if I had any baby showers for any of me? kids. no I don't have any friends I have associates. I don't do the friend thing at my age any more.

I use to be an open book not any more, it's all in the 2books I'm writing now after this my life is closed private, shut off from the unknown people that is not in my life ,it so no one cares about the little girl old me ,I'm not her, I grew up so fast once I left Roxboro ply it would make your head spin , you would think by us being on, our own that I would have been promiscuous like everyone else my age, but I had a man (boyfriend) which others knew was wrong but no one spoke up on my behalf. to help me. I only had 6 real relationship partners in my life a one sugar daddy. no not me I was not that type of person a today, I am still that way I am cautious on whom I share that with and the story that goes with it I don't and didn't want to share my life with so I protected myself. if I had no other person to protect me I have torn off one of my lips and it's just there for I don't want to share my story to anyone to I very choosey on whom I share a show myself with. that person I choose to share my stories with have has to be people that understands me. and still love me and want to be with me after I tell them the story of the trauma I been through a could still want to be with me so I have always been cautious of my healing from trauma picking partners.my wife I have now she the only one that know more about me then any one I have been with in my life she knows some of my story but she said she will read my books once it come in, I hope it will show her more of how and why I love so hard not smothering like she thinks I was doing. I have and I give my all of me and some time it not excepted and I get hurt in the process. people are just wishy washy are mostly evil. has an agenda a user or no good where find the one I mean that one is wanting and doing the same as you to reach their goals and your goals. find that you share mostly the same gods and dreams you have have found your soul mate, feel the way you do some who you do I can pick you up like you can pick me up. is a good thing for each other that the type of person you have in your life and want and need in your life?

I have been escaping all my abuser for years and now I'm done running I'm tired of it, I am in a happy safe place in my life and I don't have to worry about being abused ever again. we don't use our hands on each other in evil ways. we talk we are friends first and lovers too. Finally, being able to have a life where I'm safe and feel happy and love is the best gift anyone can ask for she is my boo she and I have found the love we were looking for. I feel we found it in each other. this is both our second marriage. we been together (5) five years now going on (6) come march 2025 " the way we met was for me a blessing and I love her she doesn't realize she was sent to me when I needed someone in my life that was on my side that needed at the time she stepped in to my life. my wife is the one person that I know is real about everything she says and do. when she proposed to me I busted out crying she snuck. out from the. cookout and went and got the ring and came back to house everybody there knew.

What she was up to but me they kept me busy while she left and came back before I knew she was gone. she makes me smile (mom) could have been telling them anything about us who knows, when it came to us she avoided us as much as she could the only time we might have seen her was if she was sliding through dropping off some food, or something for steven.my little brother, which she seems, to have more time for them me how did it make me feel. I was so naive in the head I didn't realize how bad she was to me until I was about 13-14 years old. she didn't do anything for me. this is when I had to fend for myself. my own needs I wore to small clothes shoes to small I was always talk about in school for not looking like my other classmates whom had on clothes new shoes no not me but, my brother had on the latest gear designer shirts pants socks we were poor ever though I knew how much money my daddy let me and my(mom). too she didn't do anything for me growing up. She didn't do any- thing for me growing up I saw no. money till I was about to turn 18 she said I don't have any money for you. but yet in the same voice to Steven she said let's go they went shopping for stuff he wanted. didn't care for me all those long lonely days and night and how and why you do for one and not the other especially since it her father money. spending on your son and not your daughter who the money belongs to not him at all that was my money. an crazy when I ask for, a 20,50,100, you always told me you never have enough to buy me any if that for how he come in with new shit that same day I never asked for much I needed stuff and was rejected by her every time I asked her for anything in and could be as small as a pack of cookies. she didn't have money for me. from a child's I'm not understanding any of this by for one and not the other ,I felt hated by her .how are treated badly now know I just can feel their pain their our parents ,don't want them so they give them to them system .why can you give a child what that need I never ask for anything outrageous a toy ,a ,Barbie some clothes.

I would get a Barbie here and there. but buying me clothes nope not one piece oh yea in my 10-year high school she bought me a   the carousal with the. bottoms with it, then told mama a daddy I was facing a throw it behind the dryers in the basement of the apartment where we live but it wasn't mines I showed her mines was in my room my needs were looked over like they didn't matter ,and they didn't matter to her cause she didn't do anything about my needs .I look about what she did and didn't do for me she told me herself she never knew how to care nor protect me .how was that the only words she could utter to me from her own lips .if she could have had a better reason why she couldn't do what I ask her to do , how can be a woman that let you're man 'men turn your baby into a, woman and don't protect her baby, a club up side his head would have stopped him. but yea you were not around.

I would have betrayed the person I was married to protect my child from the monster I played down with. but not in her case she let it go on for some time, I tried ever today to grow a little more and leave all this behind but how am I to do so when their damage has changed my growing up stages of life all together. I am so much pain damage to my heart and me and for that I am on meds for the rest of my life (thanks mom and dad and all my abusers). for a non-normal life. if it is normal is a real thing then I really never will have. I know you say this is how my life is supposed to be your god wanted it for me he only put on you what he knows you can handle listen to your self believe that after reading my two books there is no god in my world of belief at this time I been through hell and back aunt no god save me from all the bullshit I been through in my life there can't be a god if so what a mean joke to make every bodies fucking whipping post all my life in 55 now and I been free from bull shit now 3 years an been with my wife 5 years going on 6. now in in a safe relationship I know aim grown now per say but aim still learning every day I still growing and learning everyday if you not doing these things two things than your wasting life doing nothing at all.

I taught myself how to make things because I never had anything. I should be making a craft book of my own a put it on the market maybe I will. I taught myself how to cook, clean and organize thing so it didn't look like a lot of stuff in one space an I'm once I had my first son I started cooking more my brother and I. I learned more as I cooked more meals for us. we finally had food in the house for once since I was getting food stamps and 460in cash. 600 in stamps. so we had plenty of foods to cook a snack on. we didn't have any before then some time down the line. she would give us 5.00 dollars for allowance so we would walk to the McCoy's. and teacher store getting stuff we could afford .and that's where we would spend our money .to make it look like we had stuff when we really did have anything we didn't I got stuff to make stuff with. I taught myself. most of what I know how to do in crafty a little bit designer, I am ache a baker, I can sew I make some great quilts over the years I taught myself most of what I know, me keeping my self-busy do so many crafty things could try lost anything I like want to make the rugs kit so I can make rugs for people and sale them I know soon how I will know another craft. being the oldest person in the own home had so much on my mind as a child taken care of a smaller child not realizing that was not, my job I just went a long each day as they came I waking up by her some days and other days we were on our own no money no food she left us to fend for ourselves so once I started having my sons, I got better at making great foods and other stuff not your everyday meals and now I am a chef whom cooks a lot of French food and world cosine I have now over 50 to 60 cook books small thin fat goods sweats soups and more but most people ask for my most favorable, eggrolls or my seafood lasagna, I can. make a baklava easily and a baked Alaska to my famous, brownie. are big hit and fried chicken in oven comes out crispy. I've had to keep quiet for years as I was told not to tell anyone about what was going on. on Hawaii avenue she said it was nobody's business what was going on over here we were told this so many times not to tell daddy was dropping us off at 3;15 an we better be in the car not tell daddy anything. I don't know how I made it every day.

Living there in that place, I guess I was young and now that I am grown I see the wrong in the way we were alone on our on all the time with to supervision .my parents was as because an adult a saw how much me children needed me all the time for much of my attention could I not be there. that much crazy me. seeing for my self-see my kids how much they needed me I could not understand how much they needed me I couldn't under- stand how someone, could not have the time for their own. that's crazy. I was so busy with my son when there was the only child. I was so busy with him I didn't see nothing in my both but him we did pic outside went to bowling alley. go to grandparents' house I didn't neglect him them I had a am I was really busy he was my sick baby with yr. an am I kept them.so busy every day I got on their nerve I say even though I didn't they were small they loved the attention I gave them I turn my living room into their outside playground they had. slide merry go round see saw, bike, skate board, skates, for them, they didn't need anything they had it all, once I had my had my baby David that was my baby I loved that little boy I did I was so hurt when they case and took him away from me. I know then I wanted to be a teacher he made me feel that I could do it, my calling .so I did it from 16 years' old to 45years old. Worked I gunmen children learning center .and private child care centers. I ran a daycare out me. grandmas home for years, a summer camp, on any given day I would have any were from 12 to18 kids with me a day doing something, we did some many activities. A set of 5 sisters, I felt like all the kids were mines I loved them all girls they were but their mom neglected the man they were take not just from but from me to .and the state to them a separated them from me I wanted my girls but I didn't, have the room.my self. I would have fought for them for them to stay with me and my 3 boys. I reached out on Facebook many times, a them I found 4 of them but not the baby girls I found on fb I wish I could get to see and talk to the but I felt a little atomicity coming from her when i spoke to one of them at. but the others will be me toting up with me for a lunching. With me.

I let to many people control my every move I do or do not to satisfy them nor am I am the never person I say nor because I not benefiting me there no thought to my health our feeling, I can't get much done from other get mad when I turn them way, how can I get me, myself and I back, back if I keep saying yes to everyone. I don't know how to say yes any more I say yes when I want to. all day of growing up no one gave me advice like big mama did I learned from her what to take a what not to take from people but she left after `so I was on my own again. The process of learning comes and starts at home. well I was home and what I learn was nothing at home to teach me anything I. learned how to do as I please as I please with anyone I wanted to I had my own apartment we ran that building nobody said anything to us doing anything in the building. just one guy didn't want my brother playing with the little boy down stairs. that was their babysitter and the lady by a do her me, pulled out her gun and cussed him out told him if he came up these steps a bother us again she will shoot him.

My trust in people didn't know what that was I was so green as people call it say when you don't know something you should know but again I was hitting 12 in the coming 3weeks, what I suppose to know are 12 but how to be a kid but I didn't know how to be that either because I didn't have toys, a to, games, no books, no friends till I hit high school one friend a once I had my first son I had toys. Nothing but the stuff I made I made on my own that's why in so good. at crafts I been making my own toys since I was 12years old I had my kids I brought them so many toys and cars I at aunt even funny. I made shelves they had plenty of little mem, hot wheels' track or any things I wanted them to have. kids need a home start not as school start that's not how it works when people neglect them others see it and take advantage of those children and start to show then what parents too busy for their own kids , these things are happing to our kids right under burnoose how do you not see it ,what's happening is sad that children get neglected every day because too busy with her men .I've learned from my trauma that I am dealing with now the parents was not able to be parents for me I truly was a stake in their life .that why all the abuse came from a parent they were too young in the head not age, to be parents they were given the wrong baby. And went their own way they let her go her own with no consequence and bath grandparents and my dad raised, and my dad raise me with my 2grand parents from how to love I didn't learn nothing but move pain in, secret no one should me how to do use stuff that time or the month she showed me how to properly bath her showing me thing my mom was soups to see me thanks carol.my friend first of anything no pics is any family pics, on 100either scale of family I learned that I called family , was number my family on both side I am a child with no family I am making my family now at the age of 55 years, we raising them as if it like we got a d s do over raising even though they are not real and I am raising my baby as they are real they get toys, clothes , just like real kids they have car seats some people may not like it whatever their option an business don't count we have grand babies we do spend time with I have 8 my wife 1 all in total it 9 between us just my living on Hawaii avenue between two cemetery was spooky I was already having bad dreams with facts that my dad, was everywhere I was as an aspirin how I know Jr playing in my bedroom I heard him talking so I went in and asked him who you talking to? he said your daddy so I said it again him he said ?your dad Alvin I turned my ass round and walked out the room . I know my dad was around me lot. but when I found out he was around my son l was a little worried because I wanted to make sure it present was not to harm him ,over the years we have seen him around salt my aunt ,my grandma am my grandpa ,I can smell them and I have pics of them in my yard fourth birthday I have pics of them in my yard when I lived in nc105grant street they have followed me here to TN I've seen and seen them a lot when I'm out walking how I know how am a person walking .and have (5)five shadow at same time around her in the broad daytime the heights where all different(2)two wear hats one a short hat and is a top that they scare me at night they tug at my cover they are at my loss to make me pay attention to them it wants me to do bad things to myself I hurt them sometimes I didn't tell my dr. about all I hear because I don't want to be lock away like my mom was in a rubber room. Yes, talk to my babies like they are real them as same people talk to dogs and plants. hello they to cures out people in cars that can't hear them oh but people think I'm nut because I carry and take to my baby. not people talking to themselves walking up and down the street full conversation talk to lamp post, and walking down the middle of the street screaming a talking totem selves and invisible people so to all that I am quite normal with my baby Jocelyne, I love me.

Little girl the way you suppose to love your children. she is so special she has more any 2years olds has a brother twin and her little brother he is a preemie, but I take her out more than I take the boys out because she on my paper and there are not so when I go out I take her what you're not seeing is the big picture my baby and my juicy are my one heart beat my life line they saved my life they came into my life when I really needed someone to be there to hold me and they both did that for me the where my everything to stay here on this earth . I was on the verge of suicide again I wanted to end my life and was at my wits end everything my sons wasn't coming around nor grandkids all I had was me a work for while not friends male or females I had no reason to be here at all until my online friend told me that I s getting Jocelyne. early she supposed to come to me on the 1st of July but she came the 7th of June she came a month early she saved my life she gave me a purpose to live on why I am still here any my juicy came back to me. in the next 4 weeks after my Jocelyne came I was over the hills in love with my baby Jocelyne, before internet her am cray in love with my juicy. I had an easy escape from my first wife somewhat, but this one in not going anywhere she /we stuck together like glue. we have so much fun together we do so much stuff we love to do.

Together like painting and sipping wine or us going to the winery in the area we have about (5) thanks are close to us. The one we go to we can pick the berries that are in season.

we did the wine chucuttery boards and a wine one. now we just get the wine one can buy a bottle a bring our own chucuttery board we have all the fixing, mostly we enjoy the scenery the mountains and drinks alone are great. The cheese we get from grocery they have huge selection of great cheese. checking out all the different cheeses that are coming out very nice too. That is some that is something I've always like to do was eat exotic cheeses and wine festivals, where we could go and walking around and tasting all those different wines. these are all the things we both like to do, we don't hang out in clubs that's not our thing we rather spend money on better things to do at home and drink and paint at home party at home. we do a lot together as married people supposed to do we match each other's energy.

She wakes she get out the bed in up, she leaves the house in worried, she gets in later then said I worry. she is the apple to my apple we simplify our lives to the life of stress free and stay on our own and away from the negativity, aim reaching myself that she is whom she only can be that is the person we see every day can't change to nothing else thesis here I don't she see her as a mother she is a friend an associate I know I know I can't collect on her as a (mom)she could never be one to me so in between my reading, my lesson of growing up is coming out.

I can only except what she offers tome I can't pull tooth out of a turnip to get what I need from her, she doesn't have it, she doesn't know how to give me that .so I have to just move on with my life I wrote these (2) two books to see my growth from me letting it all go. I have for given her but I will never forget or trust her ever again for protection she only has enough in her to handle. all that is going on is side of her mind, she doesn't have the strength to handle anyone anything outside her bubble so l don't want to bust her bubble its already small and if she gets sick again she will never become herself again we will lose her for the rest of her life she will become someone else we won't know her again and she won't know me and I'm not going to be her punching bag or anyone else for that matter. I am her child that all she gave me life and then checked out because when I asked mama why didn't she say no baby we going home you see grandma later no that's not what she said. all the answers I needed I won't ever get she is mentally not able to give me something for all this pain I have. but since I have on and began my forgiveness to all that has hurt me in my pass bless you I can't judge you I not your spiritual beaning that's up to whom worship. I'm me queen and everything that has happened to me will fall off my body along with the weight will have the pain and aches be gone to I can start all this fresh my ,mind will be free, happy and no more in an guilt on me for things I didn't do to myself my shoulder feel so light now days my weight is falling off.

Days my 228 6 24an on 7-28 24 it was 220 its 8lbs but it I coming off. lol. so I knew that weight is going to full off fast know that I am letting my body free so all my headaches and pain will ease up and I can start growing up, into the person l ant to be by the way l am started to grow my meditation, my candle lighting and singing in my heart body care mental care. I can cook I love being in the kitchen, cooking and I have a lot of food need to get back in my element I love being in the kitchen my other happy space there my quilting. if I not quilting. quilting is one of my mechanism that help me calm my anxiety and my abandonment issue when juicy has to leave me I know she is coming back. Quilting is one of my mechanizes that help me calm an my anxiety, abandonment issues when juicy has to leave me.

I know she is coming back, but I have a hard time being any from her she understands me about that a little, and my wife has talk to me about my health trying to get me/my size down so I can be even more happy, my growth through all this is a good away for me it helps me to be me/size down so I can be even more happy my growth through all. this is a good away for me it helps me to be myself and not trying to be someone else for someone else. I have learned to be met. I have added painting to my craft projects. I do paint a sips at home we supply the drinks and canvases and lots of paint we have plenty we get us from different stores. I clarify.

My new me and growth a am not an angry as I use to be

I not a drinker like I use to be I still drink my wine, the love from my wife and children and grand-children we are 2special people whom love and truly are my best friend .my sister is so far away I miss her so much I wish I could see her in person she saw me from at a safe place, I learned in time what she told merwitch any one around your man and I was around her a one of her friends and she tried to sleep with my man I brook that stat up I talk to the girls mothers I told her that was my man in your house and your daughter is trying to sleep with him, she throw his ass. out a told him never to see her again, then I got to school and the gang I was in they found out a told me if I didn't fuck her up that they were going to fuck me up, I was going to have to fight them all my best friend was in the group. I shoved her in the locker a closed it. she was still trying to see him my real man boyfriend he became my baby's daddy. while the (2) years he was cheating with my friend I had two kids by my boyfriend. I was still seeing my male grow ass boyfriend I had real boyfriend after 3years I had to walk away and I was with my male boyfriend for those 17 years and he cheated the whole time the one time he saw me give someone a hug he said I was sleeping with the.

World of all men, but I wasn't. I was changing to someone I knew I was me becoming whom I am and I was getting away from him I was giving my new girlfriend a huge till later that night but because her hair was so short hair that he listens to rose thought it was a man the joke on them both it was a girl. a few weeks later I was fully myself a happy lesbian he moved out any way do to the fight and when she pulled up she said are you going with me or you staying here, I said let me grab a before I could finish she said no either u leave rite now with nothing can I get you all you "all will need so I told the kids come on lets go where're moving, she made sure everything we needed a more she spoiled me. that was my escape from

him. but still had to see him when he came to get the boys. then he just stopped coming. He asked me to marry him I said nope just to give you papers to hit me again I'm good. He bucked an I didn't flinch he step back a was like come on boys lets go he saw that I was not scared of his ass like he thought I was juju moved with him at 17 yrs. of age, I raised the 3 boys alone even when I was with him he was like a sofa in the no enter action with them except get out of the way of the TV when he was around his sisters he acted like a caring parent. once he stopped coming around I was free I was able to be myself and find me and find what I was about,
what my purpose of my life was for what was my calling how do I survive being alone in this new relationship lost two nos' she was better she treated me like a trophy wife from head to two I was best dress every time we went out every time that's how we cared our self's in our commitment to each other. Nails weekly done. she never abused me she abused her self she relapsed a departed as friends. the way we parted helped me escaped her drug abuse couldn't have that around my sons so we remain friends. I won't tear her life up because there is no reason too. We will always be friends. I escape d her habit, poison in her brain who knows what it would have turned out if I would have stayed. Bless her in her life. I found piece in my new relationship with my newly wife juicy ,we not talking about my last pain in the ass adult child of a

wife I'm talking about my juicy, my life now is what I can is almost perfect my days are great but days I don't do meds it crap I feel like crap it hurts allay all over my body .I have to take it so I can function as a normal person people don't understand how to deal with people like me don't understand how to deal with people like me they hide the truth and flaky be your friend and talk behind your back so I don't have any friend at all her.

I don't have space in my life for fake ass people stupid shit nor do I want anyone wasting my time. so I spend my time my journals books decorating designing my own so in swamped with stickers a tag and stamps and when I'm not doing that I am making quilts for anyone in need specialty order cost anywhere from 60 buy to 275 bucks depending on size. I have a 12x24 quilting shed full, to the roof both sides of the lofts busting with fabrics I love to quilt if I have a TV there I would not be in the living room it has all types of fabrics laces, ribbons, trims, tassels etc. I have a schedule in the room for when I'm in there normally can make a quilt top or two in a way I'm going to push myself to do three tops a day most king size a queen size. I just need batting donations all the fabric was free to me so that's why I give away most200 of my quilts I have 3 machines one is my grandmothers its over 100 years old and works really good just a good as mine I found quilting is my calming mechanism it's my savior me quilting I can tune out the world and I can control my world in the quilting room. This is how I escape my abuser by using my crafts to make me happy and now I do it because I love making quilts. by me teaching myself it was a great help from night terror sleep insomnia I would just sew all night and day days and nits would come and go.

I will have been up like 5 days no sleep the longest I've gone without sleep is 14 days the doctor said oh no you need sleep so he put me on sleeping pills. they are changed to a different type but still to make me sleep a takes away the terrors, I made my first quilt with no sleep 110x110 size Cali king 14 days. I wasn't eating I just wanted to quilt and nothing else they realize I was having insomnia a bad case of it. she allows me to, have my time quilting and designing100 to I try to let her have some space too but some time I want her all to myself I am learning to give her space I have my sewing room for my space so while in sewing she has her space goes most days I just run to Walmart and back home, or I go to hobby lobby. my wife's arms are my safe place; my quilting is another safe place. I feel most safely with my wife that's why I some time feel sad when in away from her, I go in the .sewing room at least 200a few days a week ,I need to start doing more hours in the day time more like7-7;30 to like 12 noon whether she is up or not I need to be working on more then.

She only comes in to tend to our babies or me showing her some quilting stuff she respects my space just as
I respect hers, I don't go her arm rest pocket and she don't bother mines we understand how this is important for the relationship. it is. hard for me sometime when she need her space or she is upset about something and don't want talk be bother or eat, I feel lonely and it makes me.

HOW I ESCAPED MY ABUSERS

I started finding myself an whom I am and started doing stuff that made me happy and finding out what I like what my purpose was in life my life purpose is and was to me and my purpose is to help children an babies to 5yrs grow and learn how to do what they needed at the different stages in infant to 5yrs on and kids life and gave them what they need as babies how to crawl walk feed them self's play with others there is a million thing I thought my babies that people dont100 understand as care giver's ,work days is very busy. They think all we do is change babies and feed them not, these are thing on the care giver list that would make your head spin. my childcare days was a reason to get up and go to work. the babies loved seeing us we were their second mom. we would get our babies at the of 6weeks old the 4 of us teachers had 3 babies each most time I would end up with 4 cause I would already have the families first baby and they want only me to200 care for their baby so of the other teachers did the same thing.

When I started work in away from the house at Gao I was

accused of cheating on the job a friend of mines got me an interview and it was easy all I had to do was go in the room a sit in the floor and see how the babies would react to me I grabbed a book and started reading it and the kids just started climbing on me and I just kept reading and the

lady said you got the job.

I was with the man child boyfriend and he was like who

going to watch the kids while you at work. I said in going to work they going to school so you just going to be mad , I worked there for 10 years ,after I got away from my last abuser, my ex-wife's I found my tree with whom wanted and did plant tree's so our roots can grow together as one ,we are one heartbeat , I can be myself she really do love me it's not about what I can do for her or what she can do for me it's about what we can do for one another, we both bring everything each to the table, if she don't have if I don't have she have it ,we played everything on the table ,we are on the same page with what achieving and what our goals are were or we see ourselves in 5 to 10 years from now she knows my one goals is a food truck she can run it, my book is now out there on the market, it's hard to say I escaped my abuser when I still talk (mom) twice a week maybe, that's because she doesn't talk to me when I call her it's me talking a her just holding the phone watching her to shows. so in interrupting her watching he to so I get off the phone. she will never be the (mom) I needed, wanted, wished I had, there is no room in her life for me, so the only way for me to escape one of the abusers in my life is to walk away from her, in dealing with the delimit of yea she gave me life but she walked out me.

Life to in 55an, why I still need that mom? in my life? is it a want or is it a need? I don't know the little girl in me still is looking for her, you can't understand if your mom is or have been a part of your whole life you can't see what I need. in my life it seems I have run from one abuser to another one, I feel that way but they don't show their horns till years later. I me abuse started so early in my life I didnt100 know anything different from what I was being done to me. when I spoke up I was stepped on and said I was lying and it never happen like said miss took his touching my arm to touching my breast .is what was told after she called and asked him what did he do to me she took her man's word over mines.

my so called protector did her job she chose her mantas her job keep them happy. I still feel she knew that what my dad was doing to me she knew it just by her tell me she didn't know how to protect me why would you have say that if you didn't see or you clam to not know what was happing to me. even though you saw as you say my dad put his hand down my grandma shirt you knew something was going on in that house but yet you didn't think let me get her away this house these people are doing things I don't want my child around or put her in a situation where it could be bad for me to be there.

She has told me stories and I think why would you leave your child around these people it would have to been supervised visits no sleep overs, I feel she say him abusing me and she said nothing for fear of him. Because when I became old enough to tell her she didn't seem surprised or upset about no reaction at all I know by the time I was able to tell her I had become sexually active an I told her he100 was already dead , she said why didn't I tell her how the hell am I to tell her anything when I didn't even know her .I only knew mama cause how I didn't every time she came by the house I was at Longfellow, school, out playing so I very seldom her and I didn't know her as mom I knew her as Anita cause everyone called her Anita so how would I know here and the times went with her she dropped us of at my brothers cousin house 200-every time soy never spent any time with her so in not miss out on not having a mom, it to the point of a should could ,would a. going from one abuser to another is hard to dated early and all mines started age 2 is as far back as I can recall people oh they won't remember things that young no we're not some people suppress their pain through drugs alcohol, turning tricks to be numb I didn't know about any of that stuff until I was out grown on my own moving around different people you learn the more you ,the more you move the more you learn , about people and I have learned more bad than good back then , my, .aunt was too young to be doing what all she showed me how a what to do, let's just say I really became a woman being around her the stuff we were doing ordering liquor from liquor store I don't mean (1) or (2) bottles I mean they was delivery (3-4) cases every weekend that we had a party then she had a baby at 16 by my granddaddy, I learned to smoke cogs fuck older guys handle my liquor so I wouldn't throw up at the parties I have had 2 abortions in my life list a kids I would have 7 kids today 2 sets of twins but I but juju survived the last abortion I got but his sister didn't yes juju is a twin. how I know because I had an abortion and then when I went in for my check up a few weeks later she dry, tells me in 6 weeks pregnant I was how u just did an abortion on about 5 or 6 weeks ago she said I guess I missed one. I didn't think it was funny was 2 kids at this time 6 &4 I was as I thought done. but my twin had to come and I wouldn't trade him for the world my little man twin he keeps me laughing when he does his comedy show for you, let me tell you he would make a great comedian he gave me that mom a daughter feeling because we argued as like mom a daughter more than the other two sons he gave me the blues by being the baby he got away with a lot, I love all my boys the same not one more than the other my abusers was me.

Man child grown ass man boyfriend I had been with him 17 years through all his cheating rite in my face the whole time we were together. 17 years of what I know today is sexual abuse and a pedophile, molester, he knew it was wrong I didn't and everyone around that knew a did nothing is a molester, pedophile sex abuser along with him, hey are in the same boat and for not turning in my mom in should be charged for the same people that are that blind and that shut up about oh in going to call the cop if I see something as a when they see it they don't do shit, %%%why did people around me not protect me they claim to be like family as they say it but also did nothing. I am so questionable when I see different people around kids I watch their moves when they are around kids. I feel I need to look out for all kids cause it is most time done right in front of you ,people too quick to show their to their kids and don't the back ground at all ,most pedifile200 prey on the mom to get close to the children me knowing who I am starting to feel anxiety coming on l cling to juicy, if we are in a store she knows when having difficulty dealing with too many people I get clingy she know it's too much for me an she hurries us out the store cuss I am starting to cling to her grabbing her hand or her shirt she will get me out the store pretty quick without letting that she knows I need to go.at home I don't have as many at home but I do have crying spell in my sewing room. for no reason, the anxiety I have at home is when I start isolating in the sewing room for a few minutes even if it to just touch something in the room that's more my ptsddiasa, people don't see the realness in pts. or and thing they don't know about ,when you try to explain it they don't get tithe question you and after explain it they ask the same it is so painful to explain something your fumbling with your self-trying to manage what you your self is having a hard day yourself I cant100 tell u how many days I go to stores to breath when its empty like first open then about an hour in in ready to go ,I don't feel good on the bus crowded either. I start feeling antsy and jittery to many sounds smells people bumping up against me while walking by me, I don't like being touched by no man I don't care if hey walking on the bus, I am a woman that can't stand man on this earth they make my skin crawl they touch me I only hug a hand almost all of males in my circle. I can feel the floor vibrating when in in the stores and no one else can do to the neuropathy in my feet and hands its painful she is my partner lover best friend life partner she keep up on me taking my meds. Now in entering a new life for us me and my wife, and grandkids. this is where I belong with her in this space at the time in my life right now in finally home with my family an especially my loving wife, we go to the winery a drink.

Different ones can have a charcuttery board of the

cheese. That is our date days we enjoy just the 2 of us. We would pick something we both like a do it. I am safe now the 55 of waiting to be here in my safe home with my wife juicy.my journaling is another way to help with my ptsddsa and more as long as I write down my feeling and things I would make myself feel better that's why I have so many I write in one like one last me 2 months then I see another one I turn in to my junk journal a one is my everything books. I have taught myself that writing is a way of me expressing what I can't say so I write it down in my book every little thing that meant something to me other may not understand but so what as long as I know why I am writing stuff in my books .the journal tell a lot about who I am to myself it's not for others to understand its formed to express my being my self-worth who I am the people say know me and they don't really know what I stand for what I believe in how I stand on different diversity things in every- day life .who talks to me that can say they know me I can tell you it's only 5 people and if you have to question whom they are that lets you know you are not one of the 5 people. people cut me off years ago I was trying to hang on to a non-existing friendship's so I now know that they were all season friends a not.

Friends to invest in my time I was wasting trying to create something that was gone years ago. I no longer invest in people on my time since I have seen in the past few years the so called friends could at least send me a hello or how you been after all the texts fibs messages I send out a no one responds I see them always on electronics but no response to me so yet another year in letting my page shrink by delete. I don't in not look for new fb friends don't need massager don't need if you don't have my number you don't need 2025 is a new me a year I can't and won't be worrying about no extra people I have all I need in my wife she is my one and only friend. today in 2024 people have gotten more messes then ever since coved 19 hit us the world was shut down and people got weird and doing sick things kidnapping woman stealing organ from bodies. all this stuff scares me and I don't like when see people feel they following me I get worry and I. go for the bus stop or cab200. I don't go these are some of the things that make me, my me how I like crafts and doing things with my hands nobody ever asked me what I like or what am I about nobody ever ask me about me .so like I said my wife's and my kids are the only ones that knows me. all the issues I have in my life come from my parents abandoning me as a small child I can't connect to everybody I don't even try to bond with so many people I bond with my wife and kids.

I was so secluded from everyone once I moved to Hawaii avenue. an had I never asked to have, was just shoved in my arms. started my issues of more abandonment from her she never was around for me I had to basically became an orphan, in my eyes. left to tend to him. like it's my child ,my life was over ,another abusers gets away with it , that was child abuse ,having me raise your child and you never came back.me starting to read more books becoming aware of the thing around me was not right when100 I moved each time learned some things that I would not have learned staying in one place sorry I moved I have moved 55 times in my life times .around so much each move was for the better for my children I even though I moved them around I never let their school grades fall behind I keep them up with their work .no matter when we lived my children where straight a students in all classes and a few tie two of my children did two grenades at once Farley an Alvin they both 200did first and second grade in one year first in the morning an second after lunch they started school' at 3years old because their 4th birthday was coming before deadline to get in to school that year, that caused them to graduate a year earlier than their friends .made their friends start a year later. so a lot of them were left behind .as much as we moved around they learned much with our travel(moving)and they growth in arts reading history very knowledgeable in a lot of subjects I keep them busy as I was teaching along with.

School and the activities I was doing with them was teaching while playing and gave them cameras every year for them to see the world through their eyes what they see that as an adult we over look, or take advantage of I know I kept my son busy away from home knowing how he was going to act when we came in some I had an already, feed the took them to practice and had homework done so all they needed was a bath and a snack a go to bed watch quietly. they were tired we had been gone all day from school go home eat dinner was dishes get outdoor backpack with skate camera man or tennis shoes we had money a bet so we were good if we need a drink while were out. come home and go to bed staying out his way, by me giving them camera that was their third eye. they sew stuff we as adults take advantage of, this was my way to let them to escape seeing all that in was going I had an out for them but not one for myself it was easy to cover their200 eyes I thought but they still seen me going through it all and hate to find out they saw it but did I expect they were in the same room with us every day and night. they made collages with some of their this was my way of letting them escape what I was going through I didn't want them to see or deal with but I guess human say they did any way because they took a knife to his throat a let him know he was going to die that night so he moved out that Friday. when I, started to watch more to I started learning that what I was living in was a heel relationship and I needed to get away for him so I started to get me back to me. I was seeing what the two was saying it happening rite in my home I was living it .and, now I see it was hurting my kids so not just me that needed to escape but kids needed to also that's. when I was I met someone a she was a huge help in getting us away from that house. I started evolving in t someone I could love I didn't know how to love me because no one showed me how I had to because no one showed me how I had to teach myself and that's when 1997 was the year a light bulb came on and said enough is enough no get up and go it was so I went and I got me and my kids on the go it was hard but they were my little troopers I was doing everything I could for them together through school and independent the best I knew how I LOVE 200them hard I showed them and gave them all my love and still do to this data.

They were good kids, but everyone has their days when it's a bad day most days they were, I to do much display in public or at others homes it was at home where they did the most and on their outings when I was at work. the 9-11 was a bad day for the use when it hit, to me it was dramatized, caused we lost a lot of babies that day at us sister New York day care center I say that because I was working at the one in dc building day care center and they were our sister so to me and my co-workers we lost our babies then I had to walk home in the idle of the street no buses were running they were stuck in the street the world around us as shut down it was frozen in time we had to walk along way home first I hand to walk from 4th and g sat down town to a middle school a high school an elementary for my baby son I walked from down town 10 am we were home be 12:30 lunch time took us 2 hrs. and a half to get100 home to 7th an Longfellow sat nw. in the mist of all this we still lost family and friends it was traumatic to me by having not known where my kids where at cause the phones in our center all stopped working so we couldn't call out an the couldn't calling in I left work found out there was no way to get home but to walk I was mad as hell that was a two hour walk, we felt a little safe once we all was home me and my boys no I did not let them go outside for days the traumatic part was me no really know what was happening tithe use what were in for an how was it going to be effecting tomorrows comings . I know after that we needed to change the way we were. living, train our self-new world we have to fit all the new laws in place into our live by the time 2002 came in I was having to move again so we moved to md and I gotten a better job ND closer to home for so the kids would always be close to were ever I worked at I. worked with children that was my calling intel I miscarried , in 2005 in my class room ,I let my director know she had 3 weeks to find my replacement.me an another teacher was over the limit of student per class and she was not calling a sub that let me know she didn't care about her staff or hr. children .I kept getting migraine so the dry, did some brain test an found that I have a split brain an even told me he knows by the way I tis split he knows for sure I had a hard l earning disability learning growing up he sent me to 4 brain specialist and they all said they would not be touching me because if they did any surgery on my brain I would lose my life I know now an I would be depending on other to feed my clothe me bath I would be veggie strapped in a wheel chair wearing diapers not knowing any one around me. working maybe ten days a month around the corner from my apt meant they told me my learning disability came from that the head-aches came from that the headaches I was having come from that I saw top notch brain sergeants that said NO.

This headache I been having a child was real and no one believe me came from the injury that went unnoticed until 2004 when I had a black out and did not know why I was having them they were a list they and headache they caused met develop vertigo a so all this was told to me from the dry, and them went on to say if they did the surgery I will never. be me again I would be a burden on some one for the rest of my life.no I would not ever want to do that to and one ever I I could never do this to my wife nor my kids point blank period. my life now is way better than it could have been being a veggie, with all the meds I take in a day it's all worth it the main everyday issue is my chronic cluster migraines those things are bitches they longest I ever encountered one waist lasted me16 days stuck in the bed no food no to don't move the covers I can't lift my head I can't turn my head it feels like it 100 lbs. if I see my laying on the floor in my birthday suit just throw a cover over me an walk away the cold as floor helps with the meds to help bring down the headaches f it's no too late if it is then the floor I will be sleeping. You can't move me my vertigo will kick in then the nose bleeds the then a trip to the err for some shots.to stop all the dizziness a nose bleed spinning room. On a scale from 1to10 me pain is on its own level of fuck off we not moving today your as is paralyzed for the day level 20 for pain. If in up a moving around at a rag pace my migraine is at a 3-4 if in quiet moving slow look to be aerated, then it at abbot a 5 to 8-9 remember if it hit a 10 in in bed. they also so wake me up yes my migraine wake me up they hit me in my sleep an and feels as if someone has hit me over the head with a baseball bat in the back of my head while I was sleeping, so when that happen its already at a 20 my muds don't work then.

It's too late to take them I have a hat ice pack just for migraine from amazon and it works, I got ice eye patches too Dollar Tree, now if it was for my juicy I don't know how I would be if it wants for my lovely wife juicy she takes really good care of me .and till I couldn't do it no more it took me one year to get my disability during covid19. my back pay was nice I see two psychologists 3 times a month and another one that administer my meds for 30 day supplies I go to my other dry and we talk for an hour then in gone and my rig dry I see once a month. For my ptsddsass.my very first phycologist told me to do whatever activities I can do that will help me stay calm, and focus on some things I don't get depressed or have other thoughts I 'll be so busy sewing or writing those thought is not there and I don't want to think about I'm alone I feel abandon again whereas before it takes me some time now I feel it200 when my wife is away I feel it I know she coming back but it's that little girl in   me that feels that I got a knot in my throat hard to allow and it hits my heart till she comes backs home .she could be next soon and I still feel this way I am teaching myself she be right back. how I planted my roots this time its permeant this time it's happening have our planting our5 kids grow 3 realistic babies our roots included them. we have 9 grand kids a number 10 is on the way.

We are not planting weeds we are planting good citizens, up standing adult. With a little pushed are enjoying being empty nesters. we have date days a date nit just depends on the activities, my growth loads me back to school to three in my hospitality of art associates in the sciences business of culinary arts and a degree in acing and pastry, I felt good about being a part of a group so large worldwide I belong to not everyone can say that. A club of over thousands of members. networking finding how to grow how100 to do some of the things want to do with food. I am about to start doing to eat everything I fix my wife will we collect for food foods I can cook I am going to cook some great food eat stuff this October for her get up early and cook. breakfast and dinner for us every day she is worth use to cook a lot operations have back off I need to do what I promised her and that to cook for her. the day I knew I had not 200escape from my abuser again I knew I needed to get out by her actions against me and my kids she left me 30 miles from our how in the middle of the night I had to walk home in stilts shoes it told me 5 hours to get home she bitch did it two times. I walked I to. the second one not knowing it for years then the horns came out in mad I made my move as fast as I had a chance my money from school and my taxes came in all at the same to.

I got me an apt a me furniture all in one day I paid deposited rent light on and got a bed a sofa and more al in Monday my grandson mom helped me move the rest of my stuff in her car in two nights. I took everything down to the toilet paper man toothpaste not even a bar of soap or the shower curtain. She would steal from the rent money I was hiding to pay the lady my bill money she stole keys pens a weed out his trunk every day .and try to say it was my son. But my son was not living there at that time. all she wanted to do as club every day. I was glad she was gone from my life. I got the best wife now the one in suppose it had I got her, we started talk after work feel for her so quick she has everything I wanted was looking for in person I wanted she my wifeeeeeeeeeee, my now wife in the beginning told me you get you own place away from here so no can come in onus income over more so that's what I did the next day I got me an apartment and

200got everything we needed all brand new. and I went grocery shopping getting all her snack an drink an gave her a key to let her know this is our home she said what I come there and some body is there I said aunt nobody going to be in our home this is urn home away from home any time you want a break from your house any time day or night use urn key.

My first time away from add was the best hang I could have ever done in my life I was tired fast it didn't. take me 20 years I know I was moving on a she was not included I know it was over when she did bring am to the bus station after we go him a bus ticket a she dint get him to come say good bye to his grandma she was cheating then. my boo juicy went missing for a few weeks then she came back July 9th 2019 that day I gave her a promise ring and we been together ever since she popped the question to me I cried I was so happy. we got married in Dec 16 /20 /22. we l played a game called get to know your spouse I made it up. how you play it use your phone go to Pinterest type in get to know your mate or spouse and all the boxes will come up pick any one you want she do the same you don't have to ask question

in the order row they are in you can pick questions from any one of those boxes you see and be honest with which you mate. we still play the game a lot just to keep our love spicy. a fun learning more every day. I was alone for 3 1/2 years when I met my juicy I was separated from my wife and had been for that amount of this 1/2 years no cheating my end. she was a big help of me getting away from (add) and even though (add) tried to destroy us, she shut that shit down. quick. our apartment was a great hide away for her cause you could never see her car in my backyard, at her house
we had space we first just entertained in from where people came over until she decorates the living room and we started eating at. The table like we did at the apt it's a smaller kitchen and so all my cooking stuff took over the dining room back

I wish the shed was over here so the stuff can be organized
in the shed. that would give sues more room in the inning room I am wanting, to cook more different food use many of my tools I have to cook her meals all my wife ask is for me to cook and feed her so that's what's imam going back to doing making my baby happy. I have realized that I have been a relationship all my life I have never been alone without a spouse. I am 55 a tired now this will be my last mate. wife

best friend, cheerleader for all my goals I want to share only with her. I have found my real soul mate I am with the person in supposed to be with. we listen to each other to resolve and thing we don't get angry with one another who would we was energy on bullshit from people that are irrelevant that is not on our level our circle of friend fit in one hand. the 3 1/2 years I was alone I found me I was just doing the motions of life and not paying any attention to my surrounding I was blocking out any and everything just going to work and home alone it felt weird I felt in some way lost in a space not know in what to do in my own place how to be free in my own place, so I was having my kids come over to my apt every day and my wife was.

Coming during the week she made my day a still today makes my day. I had to teach myself1 how to be even as a child I have never had a time when I was alone, let's see I was born =parents Roxboro=family=Longfellow=grandparents a parents=Roxboro ply=Hawaii avenue =Roxboro ply=Longfellow =md so=md Olney= Longfellow=Suitland md=temple hill md= sync=calved TN=all these places I always had a mate I never have gone any time in life with out on so I didn't know how to be alone, and I think that's why I have such a hard time when juicy leaves me for a few hours or 25minutes.i have had so many people leave me or walk out my life and I didn't even know.

I struggled all, my life to fit in somewhere trying to belong with a group, a club, have a set of friends anything to included me where I could feel like I belong is here with my juicy is where I belong she make me feel great about myself. she truly loves me and I love her past all the planets a back she is my heart beat. she has done more for main my life than any spouse I have ever had I can't find the right words to explain heron how I feel about here their not in a dictionary in am being myself and she lets me be myself she not trying to change me. go do what you need to in here for you. she doesn't get all flipped out when I leave the house like other people in my or sewing room or journaling cause she knows this helps me with my ptsddsi I, gave the name of those letters in my book a couple of times. the meds I take is the best thing for me to take every day too function so she makes sure take them some days I fore get but don't think I trust any one of you anymore. this is meant for the ones that are still here alive.im am still here in surviving in life you didn't break me it made me stronger then I could ever be so I have finally escaped all my abuser my life starts now. you know what you have done to me. gone have to go back in to details for you sick demented mines the 20,00000 pounds are finally off my shoulders. I am free at 55 years' old nothing you say to me now could hurt me ever again.

I stand tall as I am proud of the things I have done, to be where I am today I wear my crown well. now after having a talk with my therapist today and some the thing he mentioned to me is that I hold my children to high standers growing up I was not just raising boy I was rising men 100. I didn't see it that way back then but I guess I was. I just was rising my kids the best I knew how to, because I didn't have any help raising them I raised my self my brother .so I guess I did ok. some people see me as a great person and survival in strong. some of the things we talked about that I feel I want to share is that me forgiven and escaping all my abusers an letting go of them that is still here alive.

It's like a. mediocre of explaining certain thing I can200 say to him he finds the right word to fit what I was trying to say, there were some steps I used to get away from my abusers the first one was my dad, then an aunt and uncle, men, one girl, I am so strong I made it this far my family on my dad's side they are all gone I am the last on left so I can't get closure but in good with that. health wise I don't know much about just a few things.my health started to fell at I reached 50 all kinds of.

Things start happening to me. how in was escaping people that was cancerous to me. I have transformed my whole being to get away from those types of people a when in around them I tune them out when they think in listening. the first step of getting away from them was that and then remove myself from those groups of people with their drama and no dreams or goals in life they just feed off of u and that drains you of yours and have only negative things to say about your goals and plans. I've learned that people that are miserable what u to be there with them. those to me are verbal abuser if you can be a cheerleader for a friend ten back away cause all your doing with your negative words is abusing very abusive to the person your downing for you to stand tall. I have had so much abuse in my life that I am still fighter it every day the verbal abuse about how, I look, body, shaming me all those years still affect me in side I won't even look at myself in the marrow. when people abuse you for so long it takes just about the same amount of the same time to heal from it. those words that you have heard over more than half their life those word are carved in your heard for life .it makes it hard for you to believe people who give you a compliments that is being real about your looks in their eyes. I was always talk down to by different people. so my scares are deep that they won't heal, during the million time I been sexual abuse I feel she say she couldn't prospect me. that means to me that she must have been in danger herself if she would have tried to stop what she was or heard. She was not strong enough to fight off any man mentally or normally so she went along with anything they say to keep herself with a man around. her men where more important to her then I was. I was abuse for her satiation and gratification so she was happy that her men. And keeps us away from her men what type of man would want a woman that didn't never spend time with her kids or bring them around. or ever go home at night to be with them in case something might happen. an in hr. case it did happen twice and the first time she was not there .my main grown boyfriend got to me way before she did and she was closer to us in walking distance but he got there before her he was 16 blocks away she was 5 block. I'm sorry she missed out of a great girl a good daughter, a wonderful person inside and out. now that I am cutting the people in my life out of it that's for the ones that are still here, I have come to the end of my needs, of wanting, craving, and missing the one thing I will never have, I am letting it be over I no long have these people in my circle I made it this far alone I guess your god any one's god played a joke on me I was the butt of his. an never knew it, I was not put on this his shit on me list cause that's all people say pray about it pray about it not going to happen I question any.

Bodies belief at this point in my life. ever one might not agree with me its ok I might not agree with you, we agree to disagree the end. next.148ct. I believe in the science ology of it all, yes she abused me on so many levels I am now able to breath without her in letting her go out my life I can keep being abuse everyday just knowing your sleeping every night with no care in the world of the abuse you have done to me. I see that within my disciplining my I did so abuse myself on them no it was right I was correcting bad habits and breaking new ones before that got started, I was a single mom and I had to do what had to do to keep me kids out the street an out of jail their grown now with their own family and raising their children the same way they were raised. I have apologized to my children over and over I also apologized for putting my kids on display for other people. yes, everyone does it and have. done it an is still doing it you might not think its abuse but it is, its mental abuse, a physical abuse, and emotionally abusive to you children I say I am sorry to my kids very often but they say there is no reason to I did what was gave them a lot of different outlets while learning and having fun. they didn't know I was teaching them alone the way my little men are mines and mines alone no matter their age. I wish that someone would have told on my mother I do I needed help and not one person called on her they took advantage of me and the fact that there were no adults around to protect me so they all took their turns abusing me on more than one occasion. I have been running from people all my life. this book is the end of my running from abuser and running to closed arms that should embrace me. but there is a never will be any open arms from the one person that I need just one. doing the little research for myself to put in my book going through my notebooks I been writing in in going to have to pull all my notes out a put in 100 this book woman and children some men get raped molested every 3 seconds in a day so how your day going now. well let me tell you about one of my days as a child in the apartment I was to be safe in. I got up that morning got ready for the day my aunt an I was going to one of her friends shop they sold seafood dinners they had a restaurant we ate there almost ever so I was ready to go in down stairs at our apartment front door an me Kelly come out of o where an walks up like he go out the door so I step aside so he can go out the door , no that was not his plans the side I moved to so he can get by he pushed me up against the wall an started grinding on me an trying to kiss meshed is one of the many men I had to fight; so what in saying is watch who you leave your children around ,you mama's need to early pay attention to the comments your new ,old man say about your daughters. Your treating you. kids like they don't matter so you don't see what's going on right in front of you, woman don't look at things like they should when it comes to their daughter's you're going to turn your little girl into a mess by not paying attention to the signs. from my experience someone should have looked out on what my changes were when I got back from Longfellow street, to Roxboro ply no one saw the stuff I been doing or smelt it on me. your man is not doing what he supposed to be doing he is another child for you to take care of you don't need him, why would you want another child to care for when he is a grown ass man that should bring more than dick to the relationship or less that's all you want and to take care of him too. Then he will keep abusing you in a way you don't even know he is emotionally and mentally abuse you by not contributing to shit in the house. if he is a real man he would get a real job a lay something on the table. Other than your body you need to bring smarts goals, plans for our future. your money to us put on top of our game that's how a real relationship. look in to yourself and make sure your plans are to help you two grow together,

I watch people around me and I notice that no one really has morals and values or goals any more that's these children of today in messed up and confused and stuck on all the electronics and cell phones that do to parent are absent in the children's life even though they are in the household children wear and say as they please and parent don't care, they more care about their man and whatever they doing children going to school ass all out, breast all out, boys pants around them knees. and if these children had parents to care more we would not need detention centers in schools, filling up jails, prisons, with children. kids having sex looking for what they not getting from home. that's attention a love a guidance. babies having babies trying to get the love they not getting from their parents, why do people have children a let the street raise them in speaking from experience I was let go just like my brother to the street she left it up to us to find our own way.

I was the parent to my little brother looking out for him because we didn't have any parents a tall. I didn't have any one protecting me so I had to fight just as hard. We went the rest of our life without parents we are adult snow a still no prints we have no childhood memories of holidays birthdays, she made herself too busy to raise her own children. I have grown to keep certain people in my circle because people are wasting my time. with his drama and bullshit issues they create I have a hand full of people I keep a small circle around and they are all positive people in my circle. I have so many, what I call growing up steps to help me 1, meditation, quiet water sounds, getting away from damaged people, that are already damaged and not knowing they are, they hide it very well. it took 4 years of me being here to see someone habits (bad) and evil.so I was hurt but then I woke up and found that I had to get out this mess so I did my new girl told me to move out this house get my own place and she would come around more so that week I did and she kited her word so we had our own love nest and I **GREW TO LOVE** myself and give all my love to my new wife yes she became my wife our 3rd year.

I learned to love her the way I want to be loved someone delicate, gentle treats each other with respect, with all respect from us both, care for her as she cares for me all her needs a mines as well, and I know she will love me as I love her. I give her as she gives me the same, I am turning into the person I am inside happy loving a chef loving to cook bake 200and a happy quilter, my juicy showed me I could do better and she will be there when I get there she is my cheerleader and she got my back she said anything I want to do I can do it. my journals are full of me, my days my life how I am safe now. I don't have to worry about any one coming after me, I know how to save myself from damage people, keep them out my life a circle they are behind me for a reason. things I know. have grown and I am still growing everyday cause I am still learning new stuff everyday ND in achieving my goals, in my life, I have come to the conclusion that I will never have what I want. this one thing I'll never have it. she is not capable of giving me what that little girl in me is searching for all my life, I knew I gave it to my children and I still am .and my grandkids I could spend more time with them but I am dealing with my health issues right now how I see myself with growth in my life it took me years to realize that I can't rely on anything that is superficial people I clouded I learned how to be a private chef. I learned how to run a restaurant ,I have more skills in making and cooking French pastry sweets I want I became a teacher a chef mentor for about 5to 6 p an coming chefs under my belt .I was top of my classes the whole 4years I was in culinary school, I taught me how to learn different than others people learn ,the way I catch on to stuff ,I have to read it to myself to get my own understanding of something so my brain will register the stuff I am reading ,I have to have the reading tools in my hands to refer back to reading over and over if I need to that how I register what I reading and programing what I've reading. I ordered the books of school so I would have them on hand to go back to them if needed for recipes as much as I have moved around the years equal my age. sounds weird but true 55 moves in 55 years. crazy but true. over the years I have learned something from each move. They were not my places to lay my roots down I am just now planting my roots. I have a place now to do that put my roots now, it's with my juicy, we have fun together, we like a lot of the same things the wine tasting make chucut`1tery boards, talking about us and our plans for what and where our plans are going to take us in the next (5) five years. this all my growth to be whom I really am; I have made a name for myself by becoming into myself. and I have found home I am I am a queen first and for most I do I please and I can say not to stuff I really don't want to do, and not worry about others feeling I been doing that all my life no more, I was always giving myself away even when I didn't want to, no more of the I am more worried about my well-being. then outsiders they, say no to me more200 than I say it taking advantage of me so I learned that's not a person I want in my life or circle its very small I only deal with people that fits in my circle that do for me as I do for them. I am very much a giving person as long as the person I am helping appreciates my help and not taking advantage of me. I am happy now, just being media quilt when I want and how much I want to I journal just as much as I want I cook as much as.

My heart loves to for me and my baby juicy, so we eat good food when I cook. I have two sanctuaries one is my sewing room the other is in the clean kitchen cooking. an no one can bother me or control what I do in there. these two places are my world. I control whom comes in my sewing room. this way no one up sets my safe place my calming place. my baby even understands t to she doesn't come in there either, in here because there is no touching in here the oils in your skins transfers from the skin to the fabric. I needed this space so I could have 100my calming area, when I am over whelming when I say not to touch it's to protect the quilts and your life. I was saying I have two outlets to help with ptsddasi. and my anxiety, depression so I do a lot of it to stay calm for most of my days ' some days I just write till I can't write any more but it sale about my quilts me .my cooking my journal with my stickers and I got my published book my book, that was another accomplishment for me another hat. I have so many hats I wear now from my 20's till now. I am great person and I am 200having plenty of skills every day when I cook or make a cake or pie or brownies. now back about me and my health issues, people don't understand when u stand or put your feet on the floor a you feel needles stabbing in your feet, or you can feel vibrations when here is none you're the only one that feels that too. so many people suffer from this ND other don't under- stand what it's like having these might terrors and things you can see a no one, else sees, it hard enough on us as it is a now.

you want me to explain what we go through every day if you read all 30 plus of my journals that I still have you would be swallowed up in the books trying to figure out how we still here alive. my books tell a few, good things but I didn't have many good days you never knew about so this is me finally speaking up n to help me stop carrying around other people's dirty little secret. I have ptsddsai it has extra letters because I have more things issues than just pts. going on with me do t tram growing up. I have had abandonment issues, bi-polar issues separation anxiety. anxiety black outs, social tendencies, all that I carry around every day do to the stuff I went through you say let it go how am I to that when I am on 14 meds because of it every day of my life because as a child some decided to hit me in my head a split my brain into almost 2 separated piece but there is a 3-inch membrane holding it together. Some good reading of a person with all that it would be like a200 book set of about 30 book set to read, a person mind really works and what they are going through on a normal day, and what they are going through on abnormal day for you as you are your normal day mines is not nowhere normal. the situation of the mind works at a different level on a scale no one can explain nor not even doctor can't explain what the brim is telling me what my day is going about the meds we take every day to even feel a little normal in some odd way may feel normal to me but it's a crazy day for me nothing feels right everything I do feels like I'm doing some.

Thing wrong why a child about to be yelled at for, what I don't know, fell like I not supposed to feel anything, the days are split my meds I have tremors and terrors in the day time people be following me, I get nervous I can't think right I'm lot can't keep one thought in my had at a time and can't focus on one task at a time all crumbled in my mind it is a scrabble game in there. Trying to do so much that I can't get anything done these days I feel this way a lot, how I got away from my next or other abusers was to separate myself from her on the weekends we would drink so much then go out at night to her friend she taught me how to ride a bike we went went everywhere mostly to see her boyfriend's mostly to see them. that's how she became my abuser also by the stuff she shown how to do and to say to men I. pissed on one of her friend male friend because he was holding me on his lap and wouldn't let go I rode the bus (2) two buses home prissy .it was funny to us he was made. I was forced to fight a girl I won. growing from my pain, I am a very forgiving person believe me I won't ever forget how you treat and crossed me I know I had to let go of some people and for, some people and forgiven then so that my life can go on for the better I forgive and for gave those that are gone to hell and heaven s they call it they had to answer where ever they been and.

Give I going to be a flower bed I want to be cremated so I don't make my boys hurt for long time. I want their pain to be short so they can go on with their life's they won't forgive me but they won't suffer much, I've taught myself how to show affection to people I care for.my teaching to myself, meditation while sewing. this is my sanctuary and I have my shed to I have grownup so fast I didn't get a chance to be a kids I grow up at 2 to adult all in a flash.my life will never get any better than my wife has made it now for me she is so wonderful to me, she also has her hobby just like I have mines I sew, and journal, she paints on canvas, and wood .I do canvas to bath of us do it as a sip and paint night .we love movie night these are some of the things I all wanted to do with my mate ND now I can and I grew from the spoiled brat she reacted from when we first got go gather . my growth you might not think this is growth in a person200 life but after I been through this is growth for me. me being me a having someone letting me be myself why she is being herself to we didn't try to change each other all we did was accepted of us as we are we both growing up to a world unprepared she letting m0e be a kid when I want and I let her do her crafts when she wants it's a very well compromising, balanced marriage. wander stand each other's needs at all times, they need to come together and bond together. growing in side and.

Developing myself and soul for better me I have to give to my wife we learn everyday something new about each other that is good and us buttons that show not be pushed we know that we don't like to fuss we really never have thus far or argue so we don't puts buttons or should I say we try not to, growth to my knowledge as I am growing the more I seek to learn now I'm studying my books on cheeses and wines, so we can have a better knowledge of how we set up our100 dinner party something I love doing is cooking and have dinner parties inviting a few friends over, and talk and eat. I want to started a book club again it's just moaned (2) two other people we starting off small we grow together every day we now do paint n sips at our home boy everyone no kids escaping my abusers, meeting new people sharing me with positive people working on me, grabbing for my goals working on my new quilts, designs and traveling while I still can1/2 way to 60 in 5 more years so I have to give my wife all of me cause I am much older and my body is not young any more so I have to enjoy my lady and give her all I can she has earned it and more since I have been with my wife she had given me more days of smiles that any never. could, she is my nerve in me beating heart pulse. she has become my jelly to my peanut butter grill sandwich, my sous chef, my baker helper she shows me some southern foods I do regular food and French food Italian.

Food, worldwide food cooking I think my baby love my food the world I live in is really crazy cause I see and say and feel people don't know what the word mean but yet they throw it around that 4 letter word people abuse every day to get what all they can, I have been used, abused beaten and cheated on, so many times in my life I only had 6 partners in my life and 1sugar daddy, I learned more from all these people are to not fully trust people but now I feel in my 100soul I can fully trust my wife I have now, I trust her fully and faith fully and whole heartily she is a real person, compared to most of the 6people I gave my heart to. in my life she tells me what free and straight forward to me I love this young lady so much and so hard it's against the law to feel the love, l has for her. my knowledge an love for my new found person , me, myself and I realign that I am all the things I was told I am not .that I am loveable and cute ,pretty and sweet after many years of hearing in worthless in ugly, you fat no body want a lady with kids ,I 200 told you need me aunt no one going to love you .for a while years I believe him when a light came on and it said you can do better ,get your ass, up and run talk to your other inside people and tell then we getting the hell out of here .we can and we will do better alone but I learned I was with another mate before I know it we were happy this time. and it was good learned I needed to hear those words tell myself it's not my fault I can go. about life without a man, I did it this long and my young lady is my best friend and mate in all I need in one reason so it took me a long time to see some good in someone I found it in my juicy. Her personality I love, her straight forward I love, even though it hurt to hears me time, and when I have a bad day, I feel really bad she can pull it out of me so we can fix i.e. heal each other through conversation ,people will trespass on your space with their secrets that add more bullshit on top what you already dealing with I say this because as a (ptsddisabi)person I have enough on my plate and my meds is to help me deal with all the shit imp going through so please don't dump your bullshit on me ask me first can you in trust something in me to keep I properly tell you no because I don't want to hear anybody's else's drama I want a happy life with my wife .all other people shit wears on you an can take a toll on your life and health it's a form of abuse .I have to say there is so many ways that people abuse others, not know its abuse I can tell you from all aspects in my life an knowledge of it come my way ,people that always have to tell you about someone else all the time is abuse you didn't ask for that information about what's going on in somebody else's life wither I know them or not, now did it's about my kids or grandkids yea I want an need to know abuse comes from far away.

If you keep to yourself you can't be abused letting in new people you not aware of their I intentions, their life's bullshit not just being with some that have kids an u don't there is abuse there you were told to blackout of what's going on you can say anything when it an opening you need to but not wanted, this is abuse you matter but you don't matter, how I escaped my abusers I stop listening to the negative words, gestures, and I got out as fast as I could I know it was time you hear so much bullshit from people around you get so caught up in their mess you can't focus on your goals an dreams cause they are not going to be there for you when u need them they not going to support your dreams they going to tell you can't make it won't happen for you abuse see the pattern growing in front of you negativity is abuse so I been keeping myself away from all those type of people have had enough in my life , I can't vent explain the abuse from my dad the stuff that he did to me by sexually turning me into his sex toy from two (2) to (8) eight years old .why couldn't anyone see the change in my behavior , these are questions I ask myself all the time how can ?why children? how sick is a person to do the things I been through? what was on their minds to do what they did? I thought as a baby born it's a gift to carry one and have it? so where in the world do these assholes come from that. Prey on children? life is already hard for them and you go and ruin their mental state an emotional being. everything I did from the moment my doctor told me I was with child I told my baby that day when I saw him for the first time I told him that day I will never leave him on any ones step to raise I will never walk out his life I repeated the same thing to me second son I don't have any regrets of having all three of my boys. children need s what we needed presenters. of a parent protection from the world, and from people like the ones that hurt me, parents are to protect you from friend's fake uncles and aunts, those daddy friends, moms buff they can't be trusted either. I kept my boys as close to me as I could for as long as I could. Those family friends that are to touchy feely on your children. Me escaping my abuser I tried to spare my children from the abuse I was dealing with in front of them. I tried to down play most of it so they could and would stride see now in their adulthood. they saw more than I thought I feel that my oldest took on most of the blunt of what I was dealing with my son's grew up protecting me as much as their small body could. they were young and smart so there wasn't much l could hide from, (3) very smart boys. this is why I knew it was time to pull out of the relationship, I didn't know until I was very grown that they felt my pain which caused them pain to, anyhow I know. for sure because they to suffer ptsddasia and has a temper as atomic, bomb like their dad when they are made .so I failed some in the protection area but I got then away as soon as I saw it was causing temper blew up at each other it was as more the older they got .my older in my eyes is trying so hard not to be like his dad in some way that he has gained toward his brother I know they will one day bond again before I pass away. I learned from all this in 100my life story is you give out what you want back, respect, honesty, love, soulmate, loyalty and I found spiritually. in my own way and I am not nor Baptist methods Christian I am one whom believe in the earth and the scientology of it all. I have a bond with the earth. don't like shoes on when I am outside I have found on my own that everything is not what you see nor hear. it's what you don't see nor feel that worries me you have to ground yourself in what you will and wont except as messy. news, gossip negative people. I feel at my age I would know more than I do and the fact that I think differently about a lot of stuff that other people don't realize is going on in their face. I see stuff on how to reach all my goals, moral's and understanding. this world with why and how people can and do treat you like shit and feel good for their selves. all this sex trafficking import trusting rides from people I know little bite we aren't friends I know through someone I have in my circle a no other. people tell you if you need me.

Anything let me know how I can help you, they don't mean it, it's just something people because they think that's what you want to hear from them. they don't mean it because they weren't they be for you told them anything they don't and won't be there. trust me. it's at fake bull shit. their words don't mean anything they are just words people morals and dealing with a bus can't help cause their intentions is only to be nosey a messy with your business, something to talk about you behind your back because it benefits them to have something to say abuse when it gets back to u gossip they is another way abuse hurts without talking to others about me. after all the abuse live been through 50 years of my life as an adult that I am a survival even though I feel like imp still fight-end in functioning everyday one obstacle after another I speak different about things that concern my life and what's going on in it to certain people do to the statement I said about people and their intentions, I know people tell me call I be home yak ok. when I need to talk serious about something there is no one on the other end of my call. Not everyone is team you. A parent that walks away is just that a person that was not able to give you themselves to you. they aren't ready to be parents or don't have the guidance to do what you need from them I can't say that I will ever understand not having a mom why how when and what is the ground roots .of why I was the one chosen to have both , of my parents to walk 100out my life and never look back I know my dad died ok he still left scares on me for life what can a child do to someone so small to make you leave for good ,imp not an old shoe nor an ugly outfit you no longer wants you create me you gave me away .my first book ,breath my first kiss? How? if there is a god yea I say it imp scientology I go for the universal belief. a people say then what was I the butt of his jokes a given to them people knowing200 they didn't need now wanted me so just throw me into the pot and see what happens he didn't see me, he gave up on me the minutes I was created. he is not what I see so how I feel is my own feelings don't get all bent out of your shape, because I don't feel what you feel we are two different people with different beliefs, views and under-stand, what works for you might not work for me and from any life's experience I was not on his list to care for or about people try.

To judge me you're not your god you're not anyone's god after all I been through I don't need anyone that judge me in my life, when they hear how I believe in what I believe in they try to judge me. try putting on my shoes and walk a mile in my shoes. then tell me how you feel afterwards, no one could handle what I bed through where I have been in terms of fighting off people, way bigger than you a stronger than you are, you couldn't handle it, me finding myself and breaking out. of the situation I have out myself in not knowing that is what I was walking in on, it all started as a child an older male boyfriend abused me my parents abused me in their own ways of neglecting me, my aunt and uncle girlfriend /wife, now I have broken away from all of them and the struggles are and were real, I am no longer a victim. I am a super lady with powers beyond my own knowledge, which I seek more every day, with powers beyond my own knowledge, which makes me more of a weapon to other and they 200cant pull the wool over my eyes any more I have fought my last fight no more battling people to show me love, than to love me myself. how I escaped my abusers, I escaped my abusers one step at a time I planned out how to get out away from them how to become myself I had to learn how to get around them doing what I needed to do without them it was just me and the boys I started doing thing where people saw me as me and not just my kid's mom, I had to.

Create my own identity, call me by my name not my sons name juju mom   Farley mom Alvin mom I made a name for myself ,I had to stand up and answer to the name of which I was giving it took me years to gain my name again like before I had my kids , I was given a new name by a good friend of mines she gave me the name queen she said after all I been through I deserve to be named queen it stuck all my friends started calling me that so now it's my legal name .my moving away and steps being around certain people that was not good for me that was step (2-3) than , changing my way to be better I worked out I started reading more I started gaining more intellectual words and action in myself of whom I want to be joined book club to retain my way of thinking of how my life could be if I better myself and do more for more kids to help then grow up better educated them the best I could this is 4 -5 steps I took for them and myself I 200wanted my kids brainy acts and that's what I got 3 very smart young men . still working on me cause now they are grown now I can

focus more on me and getting what I put on hold of my life to raise them no I'm not saying I was the perfect mom or I did everything by some stupid book that could never be instruction in on how to raise a child let alone 3 three boys. all the things I didn't know I wanted to do in my life because I didn't know about goals a dreams until.

I had my kids they gave me that my goals and dreams. by me wanting my boys to do things as they were growing more strength to get out they showed me. I can have dreams and goals just like I have for them I stared realizing that wow I can do stuff and make goals and my new found dreams a part of my life as well as I was planting in them, I grew to start making my own so I waited till they were older in years before I got a real job, in, teaching babies one thing l always loved was teaching babies to 5 year olds step 4,5,6, all in one I took up photography at any I through the mail, steps 7-8 secretary school in Willington Delaware on the train every day for 30 days .it was in the mail to a one month we had to spend there in person for the last month of school, do finals I can type 80 words a minutes back then step 9 I had emcee, early childhood education did this from 16 to 45 years old in house ,in a government building for ten 200years and private daycares , in my home day care summer camps I would rally up all the kids in the neighborhood to go with me and my boys get them out the street, I had a 3 yr. old class that was my last time teaching I was getting burnt out I studied nay trading for 10 years took up cosmetology. For 5 months was not for me 90 hour course to be a teacher I worked with 2 yr. old class a 5 yr. olds to but my favorite was the babies. we learned together I taught myself, how to quilt I got a sewing machine and taught myself all this is how I escaped my abusers I get in to projects and bee us with my boys staying out their way so my boys wouldn't see or hear a lot of it even though I know they heard plenty with my sewing I can escape in to what I call my own world, when I am sewing or journaling it's my own sanctuary my serenity like an outer body experience I control this world I have my space to make my quilts , I drown out all noise around me a listen to my music, I get a lot don't this way. I have 3 digress in culinary arts and science an associate degree a baking and pastry degree. now that I have accomplishment's I wear a have worn so many hats in my life. I've done most of my dreams and goals for life I raised my sons and now it's my time to shine bright I really enjoyed raising my boys and now I can follow my dreams a so far I have done all that I wanted to do so I used 100all these tools to help me escape the negativity around us. an now I am free of abusive people. I been in therapy since 2004, when all the headaches a nose bleeds started they found a lot I talked about it in my book, I have moved many times but I made sure I connected with a therapy I didn't want to be without my therapist I needed to talk to someone once a week I am still in therapy today 2024 it's an ongoing process that I will be in for the rest of my life. when I.

First started therapy was in Maryland that when the split brain was found .my headaches are a life time thing meds I have to take for the rest of my life. for something I can't control it's a constant reminder of the abuse that was inflicted on me so I the functioning part of my life depends on the meds I take a don't forget I need it every day. Many times I've tried to end my own life but I stopped myself because I knew no one would have been there for my children's so I had to make it and be there. you'll way out is to want to be out, meaning your tired, fed up, and mentally ready to really be out of the abusive relationship .and doing better on your own with family that loves you. the way I am dealing with all this and coping skills, I am coping way before I was in my 20's I been coping since I was a little girl finding my way through arts crafts to keep my mind busy and not what's going on to me. that's a coping skill imp still using today through my quilting and journaling the things I have been doing for so long that it feels normal to do what I am doing I don't know any other way to be but who I am I like myself so I enjoy the smiles when I make my quilts for people I give them away. when I was coping my therapist told me to keep sewing since it helps me a lot and I get very creative in making them it keeps my headaches at a 3-4 when I doing these things when I get stressed.

My headache goes pass 5 imp no good an med won't work it be too late. I seek all the help I need a now I have my wife juicy a Jocelyne. in my life. She can be overwhelming it was too much and I need to come out of the stores to many people and noise too upset menthe perfect place for me is on an island with me and my wife with our grand kids. it's hard for me to focus most days. escaping from people that abused me are in the pages of. the book and they know whom they are a this is where imam leaving them. when it's too loud in place I need to drown them out it could be at home on bus, in malls anywhere it hits me. sometimes surrounding sounds is to loud for me to hear my own mind thinking or concentrate to stay focus some people pitch in some are too much for me I write I drown out the world. my quilting I drown out the world. the perfect world for me and my juicy on an island alone doing whatever we 200wanted to do on own space. she wood doing her painting and her ceramic, I would be quilting, journaling for as long as I want no to show, but at an did all the movies in the world we get before we movie having what we need go there for a year then come back and go to a new spot every year.

When I escaped my abusers I also I came out to the world that I am a lesbian. an hipper now being out the closet being happy I had.to come own an be myself that. was the biggest challenge I had to come to the realization what if I do or don't or didn't do it I could have ended my life. I was suffocating being in a place in my life when I was being controlled b words and empty threads tile one day I made the choose to be myself and to do that I had to make me happy, the only way I saw myself happy was to come out and not hide the real me, any more, me escaping my abuser I escaped the person they wanted me to be the day I decided to be myself, the male boyfriend I had. was moving out and mad at me for not letting him in on me coming out, I knew I had to be happy or I would be suicidal and may not be able to be here today. I know how it sound to people but it's my life and the person that was the most important thing of that time for me to be me before my boys if have dealt with a lot and they were right there with me, I knew I had to get out for my boys has already seen too much already in their young 200life by what I was going through it with me. when I away from the people whom claimed they cared for me all told stories they're the ones that hurt me the most and that I am set free from them all I can grow with in myself. I am now on a soul seating purpose on earth is what I'm supposed to be doing to fore fill my goals in my life as a wife to my juicy. I have truly let go of everything in my past. I'm free my shoulders are no longer heavy on my mine.

A beginning to feel like a new person I am able to achieve anything else I want to do and now I can have a happy like. With my wife and works on our goals and put money aside we want to travel and do things so now that I am free from so much stress I just. have to now start laying out your next adventure I want to go to pigeon forge again sept or cot, I need to save up $1.500,00 that's for the whole tries. the feeling this book has given me a new look on how people can do they think they do with no consequent sat all they sleep every day and worry about how much they have important some life do to their action we as the abused we can't sleep we can't do a lot cause. We blame our self for what has happen to the person they have touched, and abuse someone and not feel bad about it, trying to explain how you can get away is not the same for everyone each case is different so they need to be handle different when you try to seek help or be the helper make of proof plan 200and do believe away from it get as much as you can help, I felt so ashamed of myself while I was in the bad relationship that I was begging to believe my male man boyfriend how he be little me every day and started to try to get my youngest child to call me(bitch) (fat bitch). he learned early on that wasn't going to fly the butt sparking he got and the hit on his dad was to show I don't answer to that name. I change to the person I felt I was in side when.

I got away I started dressing how it made me feel inside

.glamorous and I gained huge respect something I deserved cause I gave respect to all and some was return I only give out what I expect to get back my letting go is something I must do it means lets her go too I have too if I want to heal all wombs .my cuts are real my tears hurt me to my heart knot in my chest hurt when I swallow cause I am still that little girl looking for her mom this also means letting go of her and her family that's why it hurts to stay and it hurts to go but I need to erase . having the issues, I have. most days take over my energy I can plan me don't mean it's going to be followed through my mood can feel good but my mind and body keeps me in a funky rut I try so hard but days slip right pass me I be thinking it's as at or toes and I am totally wrong on the day. I time lost and a since of the day. so no productive, happening other than my writing in my book I be planning on going to quilt all days and by me not having a toe in there I feel alone an isolated from everything so my productiveness is foggy. don't ask me how, thinking I would want to be in peace and quilt, some to in there with me I can watch my sewing shows on sewing and stuff I can be doing it. now I have to work on my projects I wish I could just be in there doing it all the time. I have plenty to keep my anxiety down in quilt design. I made myself and have most of my stuff done and ready to give away. I mentioned this because this is one of my calming. resource and writing is another one being alone drives me crazy mentally. wanting to do nothing but quilt and cook pt. keeps company in the sewing room I might put my body in and get sewing today if you're wondering why my writing is all over the place that's just how me.

Ptsddsia is works my thoughts are never on projects at a

time .I am all over the place ,even if you see me and can't tell I'm always ready to try to do one thing but my disability won't let me I am going in my sewing room and finish my one on the table .the mind of a ptsddsia person or a skit .you nor them understand why they are the way they are the In their fast has mentally ware on then in a way you could not even understand they can't even explain it to you then selves, they are all ,messed up in their head with multi

persons inside , there are multi personalities, inside, and sometimes they take over a person body and mind for me I am afraid of my auto ego ,I know she is a woman and she I dangerous once crossed .she is strong as a bull ,and evil , when I black out ,I don't know what is going on I just know what I see after mass of my blackout. Keeping me calm and focused on something helps me be me.

If I stop my meds all the childhood trauma returns in my

sleep, people don't understand what I mean by trauma, or don't think I been through any because I never spoke on it as a child I had no one to tell my parents was the ones cause the most pain and trauma in my life. I can't explain how it's hard for one to sleep or be alone. I suffer from separation anxiety from being abandonment issues from them I suffer ptsddsia do to the way I was handled and suffered around and being sexually abused by family you say why. didn't I tell? I say to you who do you. because it almost cost my juicy she was thinking I was to clingy then she an I talked some a she understood a little better and it saved us and we were married the next 2 years. I can't wait for her to read me .one (1). if I stop my meds all the childhood trauma returns in my sleep people don't understand what I mean by trauma, or don't think I been through any because I never spoke up. on it as a child I had no one to tell my parents was the ones cause the most pain and trauma in my life. I can't explain how it's hard for one to sleep robe alone, I suffer from separation, anxiety, from tormented by people from them I suffer the most because they let me down they failed me as my parents.65 I was to tell anything when it was coming from everywhere, I had no trust in anyone didn't know what trust was I was ages 2,8, 11,26, thetas total of 24 years of abuse from the circle I called family and friends that was supposed to protect me. everyone was using me for their own gain so me getting out. I had to do a lot of hiding my words feeling anxious always felt like I was sneaking around when all I had was me and myself, to fight for, survival, since no one else could help me. fighting grown ass men trying to keep them from touching me and raping me. I don't know how she would ever think or cross her mind that oh my 12-year-old daughter will be safe in this.

Apartment alone while imp away 24/7 what kind of thinking was she doing I feel she didn't think at all how the apartment would have a huge impact on my life. men see a young girl no parents around then their sick minds kick in a see what they can get away with by messing with me that's why I was glad that my grown ass boyfriend started being around more to protect me from them. but he was a monster himself in the apartment for the things he was do I to me when he was around100. just because he was there don't mean it was always good he abused me as well raping me on a daily, yea he got us food from his job a some from his sister's house doing holidays and when he would hurt me really bad he would bring me a toy as a gift to say imp sorry for yesterday. There was no way it could make up for it because he turns around and do it all over again. for years and I didn't know any better. I weigh in at 75 to 98lbs to them what was I supposed to do so once I made up my mind to get away from the people that abuser me. I had (3) sons I had to protect from the person's that was harming me sure they could not harm my boys I know my boys seen more than they need to seeing their younger childhood days. then I wanted them to see I know I couldn't hide it all but I tried. and once I got away I was and were able to help myself get well and as the years went on I was healing then a little.

Demon slipped under the rug and got to my heart and the abuse was again with my ex in the town I live in now I was so glad it was over and she was gone it gave me a chance to grow alone for (3) three year still I met my new wife .me best friend my soulmate my cheerleader my juicy, she gave me time in the relationship to be me and see whom I am inside. we fell hard at work for each other I think more me than her then she came sound and made 100me the happiest I'd ever been. she is to the point no nonsense of person she does sugar coat anything I'm happy to have her as my wife. she has given me something I never had and that's the best thing I could have asked for and that is real love, friend ship. my best friend. some of me being away from those that abuse me, she understands my crying for no reason she allow me to

do me as far as I want to do my quilting journaling and
writing my books, now that I have a best friend she keeps me
happy, when I say allow is not like you think we give each
other space its ok if imp sewing all day she don't get all in the
feeling like imp neglecting her it is what I mean, the space we
give each other is what I mean she don't get upset at me for
me sewing and she watching pt., or playing her game. Abuser
are everywhere I can't explain they are family members.

They are friends in the family I have hard time trusting

people with things imp feeling and seeing, I see more now as
I get older, there are still a lot I can't put in my book, because
I feel if I tell how I see ghost, spirits or whatever 107 you call
them I am afraid they could try to take away life as I know it,
I don't want pity from anyone. she cursed me I suffer more
than she shows that why I stay sedated with all my meds I
know when I don't take my meds I feel like I was always in
trouble or I doing something wrong when I know I am not I
am more than what I show inside I feel them,288 Amy
feelings are little sacking I want to hide those feeling from200
other people because I don't want to be in a rubber room
somewhere not know whom I am do the meds, change me I
don't want to be trapped I my own body while may allow go

takes over how when I am myself again from one of the 5 people living inside me now. I let them, take over how would I know imp not me or it feels like I have walked through a vote into another dimension. I won't know if I don't take meds, some days I don't take their and I am, lost hallucinations, paranoid, and, need, more hugs that I am getting my baby is not really a coddler but some time that's what I need. She knows it so she cuddles tell. I sleep in her arms. I have asked others people that it I been with and no was their answer, suffering from something as a child I wish I would have gotten her name. me escaping those that has harmed me I am saying to you I forgive you but never will I forget. what hap to name pen to? me how can I suffer everyday with meds to push away the pain but the damage that is visible will never heal I stuff from (1) one too many things them all but the meds I take are for the permanent damage. I hope the universe forgives your soul, have mercy on you when you have to face your maker, I no longer give you my power Torun my life any more. this is the end of the line for you, I can now breath and be happy not worry about whom was going to attack me next. whom was coming for me .and why m the target when I don't put myself out there all like most people my age I have a lot of meds I keep taking every day   so I can cope with the day to day activities of a human being function in my mental health and emotional too it been what feels like 100 years finally I can write my story after so many attempts. I made it happen for myself I am an author now too, I just grow.

Another hat on my head I ask the universe to let me walking peace and this is going to help me relax more in my marriage where I can feel like I won the lottery she makes me fell whole she checks me when I need it. she holds me when I need it and is the one I need in my life. anyone that has the mind set to hurt a child sexually or woman by raping them, is a sick mined twisted brain wired wrong they need to be executed no jail time because they have basically ruined those. they touched and they feel like they are in prison do to the trauma the no trusting anyone any more their incense is gone. if they are found guilty then are never going to change, they only look for the next child target. How can anyone do a child the way a pedophile does there, is more free ass on the streets woman given the shay away for free. Like it cracks, so why target a child is it to make you big. boost your ego. I'll tell you why? they can control the child with money, gifts, etc., stronger to hold a child cover their mouth, make up lies to the child inti making them think u you can hurt them or their parents. they been grooming your child from the first day they met your child. slick words also let me that you are looking at my child.

For years at the same time grooming them. even a for months to gain their trust with stuff, and trinkets a child shows signs early in having. one around your child you really don't know(your words this my new man)wow and then you move him in ,now he watching your kids ,the kids while you doing you he is doing more than you know they hug to long favors one child over the other ,always want to hold your child on their lap children ,I should not be sitting on anyone lap maybe just on the knows but they also need to keep an eye out for patting them on their butt or jokingly I trying to see how far they will let you let them get away with by handling your child or children ,pedophiles won't stop we have to stop them by watching over children little closer not every man or woman should be around your kids alone don't, how to understand a person whom Enflick's pain that way in a child whom could not protect them salve like small kids are and will always boggle my mind. what is going on in the head that tells them their actions as ok to do harm like this to a child what demons has taken their bring to be mushy mash slim and turn their brain to stupid making them do the shit they do to you are a weak person that need to be evaluation for mental illness. And then put on death row and their family has to pay for the images that they inflicted on the child's mental state or the rest of the colds life. because that child is going to need therapy for life., the woman that allow, stay, with and choose their man over their child. need to be punished as well, for not protecting them own child or children using children to get your sexuality feed? Why can't you get a grown ass woman? ilia tell you why cause isn't no body going for your bull shit the controlling they can do with a child /children with your words your action of hunting them more the next time. people that are pedophiles, need to be blasted to an island with other. people just like them believes leave them to die. from me get escaping all the pedophiles that hunt me I can't get it. I was a small child not knowing what's was going on with me. what people did to me please explain to me why? what? was the reason for it nobody asked me how aim doing, am I ok nothing comes from anyone unless I call no one calls me ever. people can look in the face I can't get over this where is (mother)? I say after this book I'm done trying to be her daughter, I' am realizing all this back on to the souls, dead or alive people hat know they did me wrong let stuff happen to me and just turned their heads everyone that saw in and didn't think anything about reporting it to get us some help, so I for given everyone from Hawaii avenue. that lived there while me and my little brother where there is 99%of time alone. who was there for the lonely kids in the building, no one. what was (she) thinking? thinking by leaving us alone all those years? how can a man be a man and know that your girlfriend 's kids are alone tell her to go home and be with your kids he never said is as far as I know that shows me it was not a man but a selfish boy, playing grownups games. I lost family being on Hawaii avenue, my family on ax pl. forgot about us (the) one child without a parent, it never crossed their minds to call us invite us to their kid's birthday parties.my kids were the same age or anything, so we were all.

Alone every day. yak people can say you know your (mom) has an illness or we thought you all were ok, how you never saw us anymore one I left Roxboro ply it unless we on our own came to the house we needed someone to be watching over us. no one cared .I can't even explain my emotions because I was moved away from all I knew to the place with this lady and little boy .someone I didn't know and didn't know me ,nor did she want me either it frustrated me how people neglect the one thing they claim to love and still live with themselves ago through life everyday with no case in the world of that child they don't and didn't want in the beginning I truly believe she was forced by my father to have me, everything came down on her at once and she wasn't strong enough to handle it so she had physic tic attack.. how to escaped? I have to let all this go I will forgive but I won't ever forget, my life time of meds and pains will always be there so I can't forget, you a whom you are knowing what you are doing and didn't realizes the long term abuse a pain it left on me. I can't stop my meds THANKS. they are part of my life route every day I heart you from a far as a person nothing more I can't keep smiling hen imp around certain people just to act as if nothing wrong. I will not be going back to dc for nothing unless juju.

Has a baby with lean? I really don't have any reason to return to dc that is my pat I have a new light on life. I where I am headed from where I been never going backwards always go ahead don't look over your shoulder to see a glimpse the past let it be just think the past don't worry about others for the past years they didn't care anyway. I see so many things wrong with what's I am going through, there is no cure for abusing people that still need meds and how do I know if I am myself .I going through life on these meds ,I have about 15 away some days I have to skip some because I feel that I might be able to go away without them .no when I don't take my meds I feel that everything .I do is wrong or people watching me , imp rushing around like I going to be in some type of trouble if I not home when my wife gets home or by the time she gets up. I know I won't be but it makes me see things and hear stuff I see more then I need to I panic in store and won't go down the store ales I go around to another lane so I can be the only one in the lanes I shop get my stuff and make it out. Without an attack fully blown out people scare me I don't trust many people, why you think, or say because after being through what I been through how do I ask you if people close to me hurt me, why should I not feel the way I do about people I don't know. my action when I leave the house I have Jocelyne with me she is my helper to get through the day .sometimes I need her in the house but I cling to juicy .across our love seat recycle .I reach across to feel her still by my side she understand sand I 'm happy for that she is my true helper, I play in my hair twisted more than I need to she tells me stop ,she knows why I'm doing it she tries to distract me from doing it she lets me journals a lot in living room the100 know I need to keep my hands busy an focus at same time. every time I have a bad headache it reminds me of what was done to me of what was done to me. only thing missing is who did it? I may never know; I don't even think I really want to know why or who .it was because I can't fix it. the dress said there is no way to fix what was done so me know whom and why would just open up my wombs even more I trying to put close us to my pain so I can live my happy life. I cant200 ask the right question without crying because I know it's going to hunt me I want to talk to her and ask all the things going through my head trying to get the bottom of everything if I knew she would be able to give me the truth, I feel she would like the truth, I ident even think or how what she let people do to me if she did why? Did she do it? how come you let me be abused? why did you see and.

Saw but no help from you to stop them from the abuser

what did you gain by letting people abuse me. all that this tell me is that you didn't care about me as your child. I can't even get the faces out my head, the people most are already gone from earth butt their demons still attacking me in my sleep they terrorize me in my dreams they haunt me in the day time the demons are voices. I hear all the 100 time in my ear I hate mirrors in the dark cause I see what they really look like I feel them coming on my bed at night they are in my ear telling me to do crazy stuff to myself and others the red glares

eyes on their black body look like a ragging torn up bat wings with wings scissors like claws sharp fangs scary. with

vans teeth dripping slob a blood. I can feel them when they are around me or in the house.274the ones I see a lot

of them all day

- **M-magnificent**
- **O-outstanding**
- **T-tender**
- **H-happy**
- **E-elegant**
- **R-radiant**

why me?

- why

  me?

  why me?
- you neglect when did you
- how you say ok I don't
- thrown me

  away

  love you
- why

  me?

  why me?

- how did I
  hurt
  you let people?
- you for you
  to
  abuse me
- leave
  me
  and you knew it
- about it
- why me?
  - you choose
    your
    > why me?
  - men before
    me
    > you couldn't
  - protect me
- why
  me?
  > why?
- how come
- you love men
- and my brother

- but hates

  me

    why me?
- when will
- why

  me?

      I ever be good
- what did

  I

      enough to be
- do as such

  a

      your baby girl
- small

  baby

      your daughter
- for you

  to

      as an adult
- not want me?
- page 97.

How I escape my abusers why was I the ass of their jokes on me harm anyone for you gain of power is wrong yea I escaped the abuse in different stage of my life. I told and taught myself how to get out encored his lies and stated on me. People don't know one word could change a life in one second. I struggled to find my way, I started reading, writing almost everything down important and not important. I was journaling not knowing I was doing it I just needed to white every day and everything down, now I do it 100for fun and lots of stickers make it fun. on my journey to escape I was realizing that my life would be better if I leave him so I made it a point to keep doing what I was doing showing him I didn't need him for anything. I had my own money, food and babysitting or working with a center getting better at what I was doing was helping be become me again, I needed to do better for my (3) three sons200 I didn't want them to grew up thinking the life we were at that time was right. I taught them to always take care of your kids the way I cared for them bust your ass for your kids, don't stress over what the baby ma is doing, you are better than your dad's. I see woman putting their kids down behind dropped off. do you know all the trauma that should them that you don't care about them? how you treat them as your best friend first off she /he is not your equal, not your girlfriend, not your ticket out of where ever you need to get out, of, a woman need to feed or listen to elders about respect, moral's values of one self .and take pride in their children your instinct all that you will be raising young men and ladies whom respect themselves or others these .to forgive you must know what you doing letting them go, the people that was in the wrong of what they were doing, you forgive for you not them they want ever give you sorry. because they don't see their wrong in what has happen to you do to your blind eye. you understand you have to release the power of you. back to you don't give any one your power over you .by doing so you won't have a voice in anything, they will rob you down to the bone and don't care about anything that is not only about themselves. I have learned that we all go through something but not speak upon it for help I have my dry's and (2) people I can call if I feel worse I am to call me. helpers to get me over the hump when you are in a toxic relationship, and don't know these are a few. Controlling you from family friend you don't have no more because you can't be on your phone he going through your phone, making you put it on speaker keeping you from your kids in the house with you'll lie beats your kids for control gain making you choose his over being with your kids no company from your friends only his friends call you out your name it's you threaten you all this is a toxic relationship you need out asap call home call mom dad. I learned that I was being abused.

After one day of talk shows, before that I was not a to person I like to keep busy and my hands making everything the way I was being spoking to harsh mean disrespect in front of my kids making them be quiet while he drinks and watch pt. trying to scan my calls questioning my, boys where we been what was doing, the two older boys where we been what was doing the two older, boys didn't say anything even through there wasn't not to tell. I was always questioned about100 where I been, juju spoke up, one day painted to a house and said we been over that house before he was 3(three). it still didn't matter cause a friend of mines lived next door and I said no juju we beer at the next to it. charging me for car rides. I stop asking for rides and cooked only enough for the boys to eat, he refused to take me grocery shopping. but wanted a plate of food when he got home forcing himself on me trying to fuck me. I would fight him off me even where I wasn't doing anything I was accused anyway I got out I got a pager. to communicate with people. then I got a cell phone started doing more of what I and the kids liked to do. no matter how good I was to him he still accused me, when I went to the bags practices and games he hates it, I keep doing us till I had a place and money .to help me leave even though he had moved out. I was still somewhat attached to him then it wore off and I was free of him I no longer under his words to. make me stay with him no way I keep on until I had my girlfriend.

TO YOU ALL

- imam sorry for you
- I forgive you too
- one thing I can't
- does for get
- what you let
- go on and
- while you watched

- I'm sorry

- for all you
- have done
- to not protect
- me, not knowing
- me, I 'm story
- you choose not to
- help me.

- I'm sorry for

- you for when

- you knowingly
- let it happen
- and you stand
- by
- I'm sorry
- your man came
- first over me

how many hats have you worn and are wearing now today?

- mom#1
- care giver person   a strong
- nurse
- daycare provider
- summer camp director
- mom#2
- mom#3
- football coach mom

- baseball coach mom
- soccer coach
- roller bladder camp leader
- fake ass Santa clause
- party coriander
- car register
- nursery care provider in gov.
- etc.
- 3year old class teacher
- referee
- teacher for 4th grade aid
- teacher add
- maid
- self-taught quilter
- an accountant
- banker
- lawyer
- alarm clocks
- psychiatrist
- hair dresser
- stylist
- protector
- house keeper

- chef
- baking and pastry baker
- night watcher
- baby sitter
- lunch lady
- laundry washer
- menu creator
- nick photographer
- dish washer
- pastry artist
- secretary
- wife
- secret shopper
- journalist
- quilt pattern designer
- interior designer
- author x2
- grandmother of 9
- step mom x2
- mom of 5
- artist/ crafter
- Gardner
- master of many trades

- sous chef
- international chef
- volunteer
- organizer
- etiologist

How I escaped my abusers understanding a person whom hurts woman and children you have to be in there, head and weed out the junk too, get to the problem of how and why someone would do the damage, to children/woman you would never reach it because you are not going to tell what part of the brains they use to do what they do and has done, person whom harm woman /children in the area of sexual abuse and mentally abuse the don't see it as abuse they call it loving you. abuse is abuse also100 in their life some one told them .that its ok to do what they doing to children and woman so the cycle is new broken it can go on two the three generating to stop this poison I people ,why do and would anyone want to hunt people stop the cycle you have it in you not to hunt people don't allows your abuser get away with it and you can control yourself not to do this to other break the chain and woman that's not love that's abuse I know my abuse are able gone200 except for one but as long as I keep

my distance they cannot hunt me they are not as strong as me
I am so I am breaking and has broken the cycle is family is the
first to abuse you be for outsiders I loved my dad and he
stole from me my virginity he said that what dad do to show
you love them and they love you (he called it love) that's
not love caring for someone loving someone is not that for
kids and woman to be taking advantage of them and
.children are innocent and someone has the balls to take it
away is not a man or woman they are cowards ,selfish, and
should be to death, I forgive so many people all the time
when is anyone going to say (I'm sorry)that all I want is for
someone ,to say they are sorry for to the persons they hurt I
don't want it if someone tells you to say it. you should already
know to say it on your own. no one should have to tell you
to say it you should say its own your own , selfish people
won't ever say they are sorry.

▎100want to ask her questions I need answers to but she
won't give me the answers to what I want to ask. will she give
me the truth or will she lie to me I don't know, how she will
respond, will it up sit her or will it give her a setback. I don't

think it will, to hear the truth answers I 've always needed even though I need the questions answered. asking her imam going to ask her anyway for my close ours. I know I'm letting her go and that is that. I have to let dc go there is nothing there for me anymore. I wish I could go visit and not feel like a burden to anyone when I visit she truly don't want to see media wish I had a mom, I have none she is still alive and kicking but no response to me. so I guess buy me letting the go now I have to let her go also I already erased my name for a fresh start, it 'snow queen Westfield. watch people around you.

Kids there are children being abuse every day and being groomed, if you don't know what grooming is your need to know that it is when someone is doing stuff that you not notice what they doing to our child, playing tickle when your child say stop and they don't, wrestling with your kids as grow ass men complimenting who your daughter is growing so well she well developed, wanting to spend more time with one of your children more than the other, hug to long when the child done hugging and they won't let go, always wanting your child to sit on their lap, these are high signs of abuse or count in her child out of group things with the other kids.

being mean at one for no reason, verbal abuse, etc. there is plenty of was the pedophile gets to your kids when you expose your new friend to your kids to soon they prey on single moms with stress on her face they swarm in for the kill easy targets for a pedophile to get in the treat you nice you can't believe he is truly about you no he is there, for you to trust him to leave your kids with them, please be careful before you set up you or your kids to be abused. I hate people that prey on children in such a way that it messes them up in the head all their life. I can't even ask you what if it happens to your child (pedophile) because if you're doing other children I know you are messing with you own children. Because you're that sick.

I can't even count how many times I been molested in my childhood .it become mentally abuse sexual abuse an emotionally traumatized for life, they run .to drugs alcohol, protection kill themselves, become a cutter to erase the pain you inflicted on them.it leaves a permanent mark on the child, withdrawal from friends and family lock them sleeves in their room to scared to tell on them, all this is from experience of my life. Being groomed as a small child I dint know anything about abuse growing up I found out about it from to shows 100that what let me know what was going through was abuse ,that's when I became more aware of I need to protect my kids from what I been through try to hide my own abuse from them as they was growing up .my pain was not theirs even though I know they saw and heard everything he was doing to me, from my own experience with the people in my life .didn't not do well in school due to the split brain if someone would have believed in me when I was younger it would have been found and I would have had a better chance in schools period , I know for a fact that I didn't finish the 3rd grade I was out of school them. Rest of the school year because I keep getting sick had ear infection in one ear I was home I had oink eye I was home, I had another ear ache so I was out when my pink came back in the other eye, then by the tie I knew it we were out for the summer, that's the year my dad died my body shut down, that's the same year I found out I am allergic to the.

Rain and bees I get hives bruises a weeps from the ran an it inches so bad I have to take a Benadryl if it's aiming outside and I might get wet so I carry it in my bag at all times, how I escaped my abusers for the most part sad to say if her man touched me he never would come back because either she caught them in the act but blamed me for it happening an I don't remember not thing but going to table to eat her waking us up I can't say if I ate that day or not. being bet by her men to get her on their side against me so that she would keep them around her (male) not being concerned about my wellbeing I was invisible to her.so when she chases them all off she has another one in her pocket, so that. was end #2 he took her from us because he never told her to go home and be with your kids. Why don't you spend time with your kids? how come no one ever sees your kids? I see you taking the boy shopping why not your daughter, my name for him was lurch from Adams family. He never was around so thanks for that he never had a way of toughening me. all the abuser around me the only one I could never get away from was her, I was tormented by her about my dad and what I did to her. I was beat by her when she felt like it over something Steven did I was beat for being born is mentally abused an emotionally abused by her cause my dad the emotional came from her not have a care in the world about my needs. or me period, never having a (mom) that don't and didn't want you is a hard thing to swallow while you see her bending over backwards for brother. When a mother has kids and only do for one and not the other youkan see the abuse yourself. She never got to know who I am to her it didn't matter she cared for him an all the men she was dealing with so I was in the way of her men that's including my brother, I wish I could see inside her brain to see why it is wired that way, cater all men and not your daughter, all I ever wanted was a daughter but the universe said I needed boys to grow up and be men to protect me so that's why they follow where I live now we live in TN and one in MD. I raised very smart.

Boys to be great men an that's what I got three great men, I hate people hat harm children in a way that you know is wrong so why do it you leave permanent scares for life ,it's not about the clothes you let your child wear but you think about it turns men on to see what your daughter is walking around to look older than she is makeup an getting nails an feet done the stuff eats at the nail beds and it's not for kids even though you think so just like these crop tops these days is wrong and the fact they make it don't mean it's for them stick to values an moral if you don't want grown ass me drawling over your daughter not your best friend that's is going on your treating her as your equal an best friend , she is neither one she is urn daughter age 2 to 21 ,stop advertising your daughter for men to look at you can't get mad you did it an when she come home pregnant at 13 to 20 you put her out there for attention from men , an letting them dress like you says 200a lot . from someone that's been on her own since I was 11 in 55 now. if you read my first book you will see a know what happens to children I didn't dress like showing off my body. but no supervision I could have been as wild as wild flowers didn't but I was still rape a molested by family and friends. my story in book one tells a lot. (a little girl1 grown to fast Hawaii avenue) by me queen Westfield. I am a very strong person I survive all that a ken still smile a love myself my wife to have been through all the mess I been through and I am still standing today I beat all hurdles in my way, I been a woman way before my time. I say it throughout my book many time because I want people to wake up and watch their child/children around folks cause fake ass people are out there, mom friends /dads home boys, cousins, uncles, sibling friend. it can happen it could be going on right100 now in front of you, your kids like thousands of kids before them won't speak up too scared they've been threatened by the busser, that imam standing right in front of you so no the child will not talk in front of them there to fraud for your life, your intimidating your child with more trauma, if you're asking .in front of the molester. It's 99%of the time male in the home that will do it your husband ,your boyfriend, cousins any male in the homodont make your child hug any one they don't feel comfortable around if your child make a scared face their your child face there is something wrong200 there protection should kick in asap take the child out of the person grip hug urn child for a while tell they feel safe whereas u can put them down or you can drop hushing them feel their heart fast past calm down you babies /child/children, this assures you that mom got you your safe. I am now free from all those whom has hurt me, even though I am in the best place in my life now because I am free I have started to live now we do stuff together we love doing together am winner chicken dinner, my wife is the best, I say so myself I can be me we understand each other once she need my book, she will know all that has happened to me and learn why I am the way I am the bond we have created between us .is strong and we are both happy with each other. You/we had to learn how to love our sleeves as we loving each other. I didn't want to say I let my kids down from knowing that's why I didn't follow through on my suicide issues that a weak person I knew I wasn't a weak person just because I cry easy don't take it as weak take it as the storm is coming from me .to get all I need to read all types of books. to help me stay here. after my kids are grown is cook books then joined school I learned plenty of dishes to cook I got honored a list 4 years in school straight through row I had grade point average avg. was3.75 I was the chef 'spent in all my classes I had the questions answering every day in class.

I was dressed in uniform every class and had my homework done before class and I say this was helpful for me to escape my ex girl saw me in school saying imp better than her cause she dint finish school I guess she felt neglect she said cause I was working I was working or doing school stuff well I so much happier she been gone cause it was time we grew apart cause I was moving up she was at a standstill an thought that's what I was about .me growing an she not I wanted more for my self.is the best thing I could have done for myself was let that go an still keep my plans in order. me going to school gave me an out of what I was dealing with my last abuser. she was not the person she claimed to be. I was fought me more than once she left me 30 miles, on the why, from home .she was jealous of me being in school having a job , and my kids was around a lot .she didn't like that she hated all of what I was doing ,getting away from her.100thank goodness I did me escaping her was work and school , then mostly my juicy saved me with my Jocelyne .they both saved me and I am thankful of, the two of them .that was another way I escaped by moving on with a new person to give me the love I give out I receive end it back just as I give it out she returned just as much as I did. my way of escaping my abuser's leaving the situation, or they leaving me by cheating on me .and I also use books make myself to busy200 for their bullshit now I have juicy a she is on my team and my reason for finishing school and making my dream started and grow all my experience I had to deal with. I had to deal with I no longer have to deal with anyone's bullshit it was hard to escape all my abusers, they are all did wrong in their life and they are paying the price now saying.

I am an angel but I didn't cheat on none of them .and I was not the perfect mom but I was there with my kids I didn't know half the stuff I knew now the if I never picked up a book a fell in love with books I was reading cook books and quilting book. I don't know what my goals and dream would have. I don't know led me to here today with my kids and wife. me escaping my abuser I got away by moving on with my new mate then we were 7yrs in and we parted as friends do to some events that came between us. when I got with my next partner I was able to express myself through talking an quilting it helps sooth me a keep me happy and focus on something I always wanted to do and learn how to make quilts sent 2004 April I been quilting I taught myself how to read all the different roller mat, I got quilts books .out the library books, stores and with the guild I joined as soon as I found it I joined the same day this was in 2006 so all the time in between those years I critique my own work I was harder on my self-doing my sewing helped me escape from the bad stuff going on around me and to me, doing my sewing to get it where I am today in my skills of designing my own patterns small money on it. but in the meantime I will create my quilts and give them away to whom ever need one. Ever need one. I love touching fabric it gives me I deals on my own work I can't do. a design in a book have tried many of them but can't seem to do them. I always make my own design. I have a gift when it comes to the art of quilting. cause I do my own design. imp trying to get my family tree pattern patented its 300 bucks so it's going to be a while. I have a gift to create all designs. I make in my head I vision a design and I create it I have made all type of fleece quilting. for a set of twins and a paper piece vest. I had a back pack too and a dresser runner I have a quilting shed .it is full to the brim with fabrics I don't need fabric for the next time years all I need is a lot of batting. I use a lot of notions I have plenty of it and I love being a designer for quylting.my dry ,told me I have to keep doing what helps me with my anxiety and depression an ptsddsia the quilting is another way I escape them by putting it first after me this a world for me an me alone you can't keep distracting keep u from doing what you to do for yourself ,I am set up in the kids room with plenty of space to do my sewing an journaling I have plenty of fabric I am in search for the cheapest batten I can find right no . so in the meantime I just   quilts until I get the batting to fill the middle., quilting my other calling imp very good at it to imp am still learning more stuff every time I make a quilt that's why all my quilts are a one of a kind. over the years I have made over 400 quilts imp just trying to get to 50 this year next year will hit my goal is 400 multi sides. I use a lot of. untraditional materials I am a baker a pastry baker but wish I was better than I am I already got my cook pictures in a cook book.im going to try to do a calendar for the family this way. they can cook the food I cook. quilling a cooking is a calming machining a to help me cop with the day. doctors told me to keep doing it so I don't have any breakdowns., it's to help with me being over whelming and break out in to a panic .so I would carry around a mail bag back pack full of stuff for me to keep busy, I also make pillows and my first quilt for a show sold it for 300, or, that was my best quilt I took a year to make in my quilts I use all types of sequence lace ribbons and more. Seed beads a large button I am calm in my own universe .my life is in a better place now I can do more to heal myself now that I have someone helping me get through the day another way I taught myself to control my blackouts., I do my cooking for the family I want to cook more but when I do some time she won't eat. and I make menus and it don't happen how I plan it out. I have so many things I want to cook for use and she don't want it. so imp in hard place with cooking for her, but imp going to work it out. lol. my quilting skills have taught me to make rugs from fabric a t-shirt. don't get me wrong my cooking is all from scratch no can nothing with my cooking she eats almost anything it's that she has to be in the mood some time. I cook good food. and rich foods and desserts I really need to stick to my guns on what I want to cook a just do it, we have the table back now so we, can eat at the table again. with my rugs my grandson fell in love with when he was small cause he uses to craw a get under it would cover him up. besides my writing and sewing I make journals designed by me with stickers a stencils. Those adult calming coloring books work to. I have inherited my mom's mental issues but imp staying on top of all my meds and dry's apt I'm getting all the help that I can to be me and not break down I don't hold stuff in. these are all the things I use and to get away from my abusers, over the years people don't realize they can be in the a situation and not notice it is what's in this book .imp telling my story so others can wake up and realize they are in it to you have to want to be saved from your abuser ever before anything will work if you leave an then go back then there might not be a second chance he might try something more permanent like kill you they say if they can't have you no one will so make sure your done taking the abuse ,imp only speaking all from experience 's that I been through with men an woman so don't think it just one sex it's not .they do to you what you allow them to get away with if they go off just go off right back but be worse than the man they will back off threaten them grab a frying pan tell them u calling cops watch how they change up on you.

Stop letting them bully you. bully them back and then you know you're done with then and its time to get out for sure. Abuse has many faces. these are all the things I used to escape my abusers over the years, get out with my kids and doing stuff with them no matter what people say or said about me ,but I was always with my kids after this abuser was gone a few good years than I got with someone whom changed once we moved to her home town she be little me sometime she turned a360 on me then a new mate showed up 3years later an she was an abuser as well found out 4years in after being there for 3 1/2 years before the monster showed up. And I was glad when it was over and gone I was glad a so was my girlfriend/ wife. the wife I am over the head in love with a loves so much .my juicy she is just the butterflies I feel every day when look as her, she is my sweet heart, she is so sweet and silly to me makes me so happy. the tree years I was so alone gave me a chance help myself developed getting my identity back to whom I am. I am queen Westfield ,I belong here with my wife she is amazing person, my cheerleader now whatever I want to do she helps me get there, I can say start by finding whom you are what goals do you went to reach I did these things an now I 'm retired teacher an on disability chef ,baker, pastry artist and I got my associates degree all in. 4to 5 years ,this book is part 2 how escaped my abusers by using the tools have shown you in this book created my diagram of how many hats I have worn an hats I'm wearing now and still gaining hats I'm wearing and earning today I listed my achievements too. I know if I can do it you can too.me becoming a chef was one of the greatest achievements for me knowing how I love to cook and make stuff I love doing this in between sewing and journaling, my food warms the heart as much100 as the bellies. I want to do me exotic foods for my wife she loves my food I'm back cooking like I was when we first started dating I said I all cook for you that all he asked me to do in the relationship.

All this helps me with my anxiety that I suffer from my depression cause no one can control it but me. it's my world just like quieting, journaling no one can come in my space and tell me how to do what I do. I recognize some of my triggers, my triggers so I avoid 200them as much as possible by staying up beat and away from those whom triggers, my experience of what I deal with, things that feel like I need to leave the area its best I get out of the way there not good for me at all. me staying away from triggers and negative people that talks a lot but doing nothing or going anywhere with no goals. and dreams I found group I like seeing once a week out to have a 1o min talk about my quilting it helps me to have a quiet and I love being on my own planet that's what I call my sewing an.

Journaling I feel can't nothing touch me I was in control of what goes on in there my peace room quilting this keeps my drive of quieting fun and coloring adults coloring books. I design my own quilts designs I can't copy other people designee. I can only do my stuff the quilting is my savior when I'm quilting my fabric talks to me tell me where it wants to go. I know how I can manipulate to my design l have over 200 designs I need to make for my show I want to have at the museum an then maybe I can havea3day show of just my quilt s I can do a lot of ropes and need a bags of batter the large bagel so I can make them all .I speak through my quilts I show my love in end one I make I take pride in my work .I have some days where I can't design at all but my wife push me so I can control my ptsddisa, and my nerves calm down, of carry a headaches and my nerves calm down, at carry a headaches. Every day of my life most days it's at a 3-5 anything the 5 is causing my migraine to a 6-10 and those are stronger, and they crippling me where I am struck in the bed for anywhere from1to 10 days in the dark then the longest one I had was 15 days long in the dark. and a quiet room can help me relieve my pain and once I go through it I can't talk or move so they can subside back to a 4 -or3 that's where I can have a normal day

All these things in talking abused are my helper for staying in control of my anxiety. depression and my other issues there are many things you can help control your issues you have to find what works for you. just like I did and I am so happy being away from the abusers in the past. but I keep my mind looking forward since I have for given the people my past imp free to be and do as I please my wife lets me be a big kid. when I am she like a let of the same things so we. both are care free in our relationship we give each other room too grew while we grow as each other .and as one, we have some of the same taste idea's and creativities we are us we are working on us getting her a food truck and us just growing together .my question on all this is why me? I can't ask this question enough why? was I chosen to be the whipping post for (2) parents? they must have hated me from the beginning? I was the laughing stock of the family they all knew (mom) Anita was how she was and the me stay there never once asking are you ok. all I try to do to close to her when I'm around she pushes me away; I have to go on with my life. and let her truly go family can be mad at me or they may be understanding. how everything feel will not change my way of letting her. go I never had her in the beginning so why keep trying to get her now I am losing nothing you say how can I be this way /task you did you, 120 read my first book? the lady that. game birth to me did not raise me she abandons me a very young girl and want on and have another child she raised tile I was 11 he was left to ne to raise. and I lost my childhood!!! I am being a grownup living my childhood now with my hot wheels, dolls for Jocelyne stickers. (Lisa frank), I love the color they make me smile .me getting myself to a point in life where I am happy, and leaving all this behind as much as possible the scares no memories. I am never going to forget but100 I do forgive. The person that did stuff to me just made me a stronger, how I am today cause. what was done to me I am a strong person I could have a slew of babies etc. I choose to not put myself out there in that way in some words you can say I was green about a lot of things do to no guides I learned from others I took a bit of this person a bit from that person and I grow off their being and doing that how I can be as strong as I am now.me finding out whom I am now since am free from harm 201,i am able to grow and be happy and my relationship will get better the more I am healing the more I can let my wife in she knows some of my life story but not all I afraid to share with her that part of my life now since I am come up parts here and their but never or sit .down fill blown out tears explaining my life.

When she asks me. but she never asks me anything she see me cry she comforts me all the night terrors I have night rammers, my night terrors are attacking me. she holds me pull me out my dreams she is for much my strong supporter she not playing when it comes to me and what I try to do inspires me to try it she is the best thing for me, I search deep inside myself to understand the people that like to cause pain on others to make themselves, look good to for fill their own insecurity or power of controlling someone pedophiles are more100 men than woman 90% is men 10% woman that are pedophiles most of the time its right in front of your eyes but you won't or can't see it but you won't see it cause it's your man or your girlfriend I hid this for years from family so no one would get hurt and them reading my book, will see the truth ,of what I seen done and be through this is not a pity party its way from that ,it's a way of me letting go an moving on .I am not the person everyone saw me grow and the year they missed I found out how to go without a lot of things200 but I learned I am not to hold on to no one and nothing people walk in and they walk out so you can't hold everyone for everything just the ones that wants to plant roots with you to your family tree I have a small family tree that's all I need ,I let go of others for reasons they know and, I not going back on my word once, m done you no longer mean anything to me I am moving on ,no more tears for what will never happen no more tears for what I. no longer wanted ,no more tears for someone that don't want me ,no more tears our love lost, never was there. I am and always will have that in the back of my head I was born and never wanted it a closing that file in the burn file section of my brain, you can't cry for strangers, people that don't matter, won't matter and to people who matter won't mind or be worried and people that don't matter who cares your feelings are irrelevant to me about me. choices people looking in a mirror and can't see the wrong, in themselves100 but points and whisper about other I am caring, loveable, smart, honest, sweet, now icon share me with my one and only juicy, and our 5 kids 1 girl 4 boys 9 grand kids loving a person is more than any amount or thing it's a beat of (2) two hearts beating together as one you inhale they exhale that's love she see wow and all. your flaws are my flaws and my flaws are your flaws that's love they make the person their character, personality makes them with their mind. 200set.someone you both see you can grow old together that one person that makes you smile. laugh, and knows your heart is pure, I am an open book about my life and any one ask I'll answer., not saying they will or will not like what I say but I have always been an open book. I have no shame in my game as you say I will have my dream life now I can cook and quilt allay if I want to this is me dream to share with my baby and cook food allay I have the most pleasure quilt time when I am sewing or cooking, starting in sept, we will be selling plates, I happy that we are finally. going another step start building up for our food truck. we want a food truck to go to the factories and sales our food .food for me fills me up when I cook I feel joy to see others eat my food .ND when I make a quilt and give to someone .one of my quilts and see their faces of happiness to have a blanket all to their selves .where they can write their name on it once I started teaching my self-quilting I had a new calling .when I started it , I saw the smile s on their faces and that drives me ,to make more quilts I drive hard on my design's I created so many design 's I made myself. I just need to cut up a lot of fabric. For any one that I am going too rate need more small sizes to use them.as a person that suffers from so much mentally abuse c-ptsddisa me having all my sewing stuff .an journaling help me manage my emotions and other things like migraine if I can focus on one thing at a time in any time of the day, I need help some days to get jump started because my c-ptsddisa kicks in as imp getting up for the day all this put on me over the years help ,shouldn't have been there I missed a lot so it's hard to swallow all this every day I struggle with thinking about taking my own life everyday cause I can't get of the meds I can't get rid of migraines that won't ever leave me so it's hard to forget those whom hurt me , my down days are more than a few .I have love for everyone no matter how much people hurt me I still try to see any good in people, no matter what I can't hate cause it's just not in me I forgive than I should, but since all the abuse is gone and now I can help some other people by reading my books, I tell anyone that is going through anything like I have been through that it would help them. see that there is a light at the end of the tunnel of a happy life out there once they get away from the person that hurts or are controlling and hurt like I didn't and by reading this book can get some help from someone soon family a friend hide at a neighbor's home till someone comes to help you get away please believe me you can get help, we are out here to help you live your best life. you can do it I now you can contact someone you trust some on will be there for you all you need to do to ask someone to help you tell someone. I didn't have anyone to tell or talk to cause I thought what I was going through was normal and it was not but no one was there to be my protector, if I could help I will help none living in these situation. I can talk to people and mentor, very god to others and I am a great ear when someone needs too talk so I feel that, that's my other calling helping people deal with things they sure going through l hope my two books reach one person a move. I have done good, for my children and woman of the world someone needs to help us children and our woman from being danger for life.

My saving myself and getting my kids away from that abuser the sooner the better so I did once I saw the light a bulb came on in top my head. I ran my kids with my first girlfriend. I was good until I met my first wife in TN. i was in an abuse relationship it took me 3 years getting from her at the end of our married 7 years she had cheated the whole time she fought me on more than occasion. I moved out of the house we shared tile I met my now wife she thought I was still living there but found out that moved out and got me a place for me and my juicy to be there with me more so we created our little love nest.my wife is special, my best friend my cheerleader on anything I want to do. I have everything almost I could ever want now a great wife sale of grand babies and 2 more kids so now I have 4 boys and 1 live daughter a 1 realistic born baby girl and boy. all the schooling I was doing our 5years she made sure I stayed on top of it even when I felt like I can't go anymore she made sure it was done no matter how I felt she said you are almost done you can do this, yes I can finish an I did I finished on top my son am was with my doing my first midterms helping me get the task done in 90 min he was going through all my task papers looking for the answers it was open book testis was on it all of my classes I am thankful they all pushed me to finish I have 3degrees now thank family for helping me when I was weak. I waited this long to fore fill my dreams. of what I wanted out of life a now I have i.e. wanted to be a cook I say that because I didn't know the proper name for it was chef pastry artist baker I am a culture chef which means I can cook foods from other countries and their baked goods. I am a baker I can make the most difficult desserts like a baklava, lava cake, baked Alaska, osha cake, sticky buns. I did all this after my kids were grown an on their own. they are proud of me they told me so. what I did I was lost for years trying to raise my boys the best I could I did it alone a when I say alone I did have their dad at all helping their grandparent didn't help either my(mom)didn't help me either I had no one come by get my kids for the weekend take them for summer time holidays this was all me I didn't have a village like the rest of you all I just had me. I was my own village for me and my boy's yam so what I had a man living with us in my grand mas house that's all he did live there he never did for my kids if he did I have to pay him back so I never asked him for a penny. He was there like a piece of a chair or ottoman but nothing else. I wish there was a Manuel for the raising of the proper children nope there is not one book on it you make it work as you go on in life raising them you learning.

Just like they are. They didn't have the best but they had wat
they needed an a little more what I could buy for them I went
without all their life just so they could have it, they had clean
clothes shoes on their feet a food in their bellies they had
snacks to but no candy. they had way more than I
had growing up games bikes skate's roller blades scooters you
name it they had it all the video games they wanted a toys
since I was a babysitter at home I was bringing in me
check 495.00 child support a watching kids I was 800a week
they were at toys r us every weekend getting some thing
an maybe toy stores getting what they wanted, as a safe and
happy me I can now relax and work on myself she is a great
person given me the I need to work on myself that's why she
gave me the third bed room for my crafting a sewing to
share with my babies I am going in my sewing craft room
every morning and I quilt as much as I want she peeps in
on me but don't disturb me unless we are going somewhere. I
need to be in there more but I have other obligations first
I am blessed for her, helping me heal from all the damage I
'am struggling with that I told her about she told me she
will never leave me. we will go through whatever it is
together. I felt like I was going to be alone again when I was,
getting ready for my operations I've had like others have
done to me shies a real wife and true partner. She was with

through all my appointments in the lobby of the operation.

Room 5am waiting for me whatever time I had to be there she made sure I was there or each operation and my doctors are in chat, Ottawa TN, I have an operation covering up and she is taking me for that one two I have never had life partner that care this much for me .so I know she is real, she is my right arm to my left shies my rain drops in the sun shine she catches my tears when they fall. she is a truly loving person. inside she is my hero super woman to me I have the best, escaping my abuser is not just one thing you're doing your letting of bad energy an bad environment you are rediscovering yourself you are growing stronger every day you see that all the lies they have told you to make you stay with them is move damage you have to huddle over to see clear roads in front of how you are becoming someone special to yourself ,you see the real you and your start loving yourself more, and doing more things just for you, the new roads you are about to in bark on will be great moves and paths to new things jobs offer maybe school just know that whatever you do you're in control of it do go back nor look back there is nothing back there you want, your free to be yourself you earned the right as human being to do as you feel just be a good citizen along with being able to breath and not being controlled by someone that don't love you if someone truly loves you should never abuse you. I am I guess saying my own testimony, how.

I found me and found true love and in my escaping I didn't bring any thing from my old. partner in my new life with my new wife you can do it just have the strength to walk away or run away and please don't stay for the children get you and your kids and run the longer you stay with the abuser the more damage they will be by seeing you being abused they start taking on those bad habits and they will be angry all the time and family did help me get away. our help comes from many places in life no matter what or time you need them. You start over, it's the not starting that holds you on to an be stuck in the abusive relationship I deserve much better and I now have the someone that loves me. all the love all the mess my abusers told me verbal believing until I started doing owing stuff with my children and not include the guy at just sit around like a chair my children and I not including him was my first steps, my children and I not include him once I started keeping off my children and I out of my grandma's house, until they were ready for shower and bedtime. He (there step dad) would ask about dinner we already ate earlier before sports practice the stop doing for us so, I stop cooking for him I had to show him. I didn't need him once he saw that I was very independent he got scared, because he could no longer control me in his head but he never had control from the jump .it was that he was all I knew as far as a male boyfriend so I steed because I thought that was love, it nowhere near love he loved himself more than me and the.

Children he us to sit the house 24/7 365while he was out cheating on me the whole17 years were together. buts not what we wanted for selves. he would drink his beer and watch TV. but we didn't want that no nor did we listen, your /my abuser used things against me like he charged me gas money to get food for all of us to eat, when he was eaten just as much. but I started shopping and bring out grocers in house without this help he accused me of sleeping around. I took his verbal abuse and constant rapping's for years the mental abuse was starting to affect my children yes17 long years in my life was wasted on him of no plans for tomorrow or even 5 years from now don't stick around after 5 years if he doesn't commit to you. he stated cheating with a friend of his friend the hooked the two of them up the abuser will separate you from friends and family .so if you are dealing with some of the shit I went through you need to leave him/her now it only gets worse ministries but he couldn't we lived in my grandma basement so I was home I still doing me because I was home you was living there for short time any way but it ends up being 17years and not the 3 you all agreed on. Family is there for you don't defend your abuser he will do it again as so as all get home I can tell you from experience that I ran so fasten so far never looking back over my shoulder ever again. her family may not seem like they care your wrong they. done like him they can see bull shit walking write to you they warren you not listen to them cause you think he loves you he don't ,he say it for you to stay don't fall for his shanagins.i ask myself with all the freedom in the world why did I allow it for so long first off I was 11 1/2 when we started dating's no I didn't know anything else until that light bulb came over my head this is wrong get out now .I stared my escape day by day acting like nothing was wrong until I could get me and my children somewhere else to go no body that abuse you /or me l loves no one but themselves hey say it to out to make you stay with them ,after my dad the 17 year was here he did it for 6 years (my dad) I hung with my aunt I had a very well vocabulary towards mint get what want from them an ill get it cause they want they wanted that cat ,she abused me by having me do what she was doing I did me times an out her times I said no I didn't want to it, it's wrong for 16-year-old to teach son eight-year-old the stuff I know now as adult I had men 8 to 24 buying us stuff on the weekend bring drinks so we could party on the was al love the place rubbing lotion on my legs and arms because I told him to he was derrick like my little pet he did what eve I told him to do he did it, I was taught how two fuck in the third grade an I.

knew. I use to go to store buying beer .and cogs, had no age limit on it like it does now, we always played truth or dare if u ever did I lost the third go round in truth or dare I was dare to sleep with him that night so my aunt knows to never ever dare me to do shit cut she knew I am not scarred of any challenge back then I was the little rose u cross me or say something out you wrong to me out your mouth cause this little rose would fuck anybody up on the block knew it, so that mass party that year I fucked under the front of the gifts under the tree then when it was over it was like high 5s now you're in the group with us now u say anything u want aunt no body going to much with you, everybody already I was a little rose so I had to be a bad bitch hanging with then they knew to don't say shit twisted to me .we had parties every weekends ,I been drinking since age 2 granddaddy (b)would give me a cup of his home made eggnog and at parties I was the bartender so I knew how to mix drinks an smoke cig down on Longfellow we didn't have rules on Longfellow we did whatever we wanted to do an so did my children she wanted them to just run through the house , I wrote this book to love myself again find me . separated from the boys as my name always from tizzy ma alma jimmy want my name to be known as I am not just a mom my name is queen. don't get it wrong.

I love my young men but now I me again and grow up

it trying to be blessed to have my wife and another I saw it's not the same as having your own those days I wish I had and other days I am glad I don't and didn't feel raised myself to be good person. then I got hurt so many times by people I pour my love and heart in to. burn me in the long run I can't understand how I end up why all the cruelty. Toward me from anyone that's why my faith is none existence. I washes joke to the world to grow and not be loved .it must be written on my forehead so I believe in non-existing person, or anything pepo try to push down your throat their bible thumping ass knocking on people's doors 8am till about5pm. go somewhere sit down stop pushing what you interned from that book. Not everybody interned stuff same as you if we all felt the same walk the same at the amen what are we will tell u we are puppets been danced around by one person pulling all the stings. I am not Pinocchio am me an individual human being an I see the universe is given my all the answers I need just look around you people we living with robots a deadly disease they keep just popping up oh a no body knows where they coming from, universe is my answer in a ScienceLogic just not getting I too it on my own no group thing just talking about my own way of learning something new for me, no body deserves what I went through from anyone I did not deserve to be abuse on you mistakes we did ask. to be here but as a small child that can't defend their selves from grownups either but my life has been erupted so many how can I believe in anything or anyone I feel and truly believe in earth I closer to earth ataman anyone that wares shoe we should not have restricted you on between earth and you. you get most of your minerals from mother nature earth that why dot like shoes. Unless we going somewhere. my escaping from so many people in my life I can now say ii am happy idly life no all the season I been through it was 6 storms I been through an season7 is the best one for me it perfect either here. there will not be any more seasons in my future. I am over static it seasons (7) seven she feels the same way we are in our last season change. we are each other's autumn. we don't need nor want any other nor want any other season, we read on the same page in u

marriage. We complete each other we fit the (2) piece puzzle in a puzzle box together. my freedom from my abusers is a blessing it taught me a hell of a lot about people and when they show you on day one their true selves them, that a sign of either you going to talk it or you going to keep it to yourself about how to do or get away I can talk about it because I have done he didn't show her real side tile 2 days after the wedding that was5 yeas in .so year in healing from the true her showed up, aim healing from it all so

I won't hold on to it. anymore in this marriage so these2 books tells it. all about me and my pass so I am glad it's over no more stress no more season, people I can strive more now since in in a good. marriage to my wife juicy I hope that others can escape the person abusing them kids and woman to a safe place. I read my emails daily my email is alvinabrooks157@gmail.com if someone wants out I. can try to help you with growing of my resource team to remove you from the situation. in every relationship was cheated on I never did any cheating I am green with the signs growing but at my age now I see bullshit a mile away now so I go a different road so that's why I'm glad I am and have my new wife juicy we are silly together I love her in words that don't exists. I have a great song we played at our wedding I sewing to her and she sung one to me, I fear fora lot of children just by their surroundings at home with their siblings a parents. that don't have the intentions in their kid's best intention in their kids then more into their children that's when the most damage is done. in house with parents homes the children should come first you children come first you gave birth too. being with someone from 11 1/2 to 27 is my whole life the person was much older should have known it was wrong at the beginning but didn't change what he was doing with me little girls need their dads to grownup with real love except me he.

Took away from me I clearly can never get it back or give it away. the years we were a common law marriage 17 years everyone that didn't tell n him to help me, are all pedophiles because they know it was wrong and let it just keep going knowing that we were without parents but I had a grown ass boyfriend at my age and didn't see or say anything no one called cps or ds nothing soon my eyes and you just as much a pedophile a she is. escape from under his spell I Dall it I only know of him in my life he took advantage of child and does the things he did to I was a drinker because he was always bringing it our home every day and having sex some days more painful than other him forcing himself inside me really hard while holding me down forcing his self in my mouth giving me alcohol at to 18 was illegal but like I said I didn't know and before did nothing I don't know how he can sleep right after all he has done to me sexually. Statutory rape. molestation, mentally, physical emotional how can someone do what he did to me. yes, I was a child legally couldn't. consent to sex all those years. I don't trust men period; I don't like their smells a body is a huge turn off to me, do anything for me 250it a whole person turn off. I give my all even push myself Tobe her daughter it's almost as if in pushing myself on here why? She is never going to give me what I want (ammo) shunt and will not ever be that to me.

The damaging is a life score in my heart even through

I gave my all to everyone, I don't need. and didn't get it in return. people don't love you as much as you love them, I found my love when I found juicy she been hiding up until now I had to move to **TN** to find my love. how I keep saying I'm letting go but all I want will haunt me for my whole life cause no matter how many times I try to fix myself (on days) that day will never come. me ever having (?mom) why can't I have what everyone has a mom she had one but separation myself from the family since it's not mine had to create my own to have one have given some one forgiveness of what they have done to me or let things happen to you is a growth is you to know that they are not able to apologize they can't see nor except that they cause much harm to someone the claims to love let abuse happens in front of them and they still won't say if ever though they see it and know it if you tell then and you still don't do or say in sorry .if I can get that I would know she recognized she wrong, and then come in to be ammo to me right now we are associates and that's all but I know deep down she is suffering from something too she so bottled up I can't be around her as much as I want it's sad that I have to end what little relationship I have with her but to heal properly I must let go of .her in my life these last pages are things I needed an wish I had could say to her these are things I wish she , would answer for me I know her explosion she have every 10-17years apart done so she can still tell me my questions she won't she is holding back she knows the answer but won't tell me the truth .I can't tell she if telling me truth or is it a lie. I am asking her I she my real my real daddy or not? why you couldn't care about me? or for me? what I do to you but be born. You, you choose to have me I didn't ask too, believe it or not you chose all that

for me or didn't want me why? You create me? why count
you love me or even like me ?3days after I was born you were
in the hospital for a breakdown psychotic and we meaning
me and you were separated for while fee weeks could have
been a month or two. then you left time and went to have
another baby on my daddies cause all never divorced him,
then out second child you went and had with another man as
you rid him tile was 5 then out choked out n left all
responsibility on me tile you put on me. you had you second
child to raise him tile he was5 and it was like you fell off the
sides of the earth you left him in my care tile I was put out
the apartment over what his girlfriend's lies and then found
out she was lying you never apologized to me about that
bullshit, you have 9 grand kids a don't feel anything for them
or bout them hr. is not on pic of you with them at all and
I have.

One with mama beautiful me a you to show the five
generations, jar was missing in the pics. it's a shame she lost
this side of her family for some men to become before us we
have great children a grandchild she doesn't ever see talk to
or spent time with, their grow now and have children of
their own and you are missing out on them growing up. an all

the stages of life. how can woman put their man in front of their kids when it's about time for your kids when it comes to dinner if he working 60 ,70 hrs. a week then yes he gets a plate made for him first then the children was raised he gets the first plate then you kids ate, how can a parent can't take care of a child/children you should think twice
about protection. married or not swallowed they pill you don't want your child, why not give your children / child away cause at this rate you are messing them up in the mind mentally and emotionally because they be better. don't get it or me wrong some time things change events happen out of your control or was it in your control a you froze and did nothing. Hats when you use protection, children are not in the decision making when you're the ones fucking making then if you don't want them than use protection, I am child of circumstance that was not in my control. I knew for each time I get pregnant I was going to be in my kids' faces
.at all-time all up in their business everyday letters a note I found I read, my children's business was my business too., my children in a way was a huge lesson and a curse at the same.

Time for some but my children were **NEVER EVER AN ACCIDENTS**, never that, they came when I need them to come in to my life. they saved me they gave a purpose. there was time a few, I wanted to check out because I didn't have a clue nor was I perfect I, made I know a lot of mistakes but they- never been in jail tile dumb shit do dumb shit happens, but one to (2) two hrs. they still don't have a record but a lot of ass whipping to keep them in line my children are very smart has a lot of different skills as adults and they are teaching their kids to be up standing adults no bad rep, I keep after them to story out trouble. I was what the guys in the corner store call me (mean mama) that was my other nickname. thy would call me because I was always on my boys I am- sorry I could not give my kids all that they wanted I couldn't afford much with 3 boy raising alone. but you see my children was there with me through easy and the struggle we did it together. yes, some may say I'm still bitter our not having a mom, yea it hurts but I can't cry any more tears over her not wanting me. I am new starting to be happy, I have to stop calling for after this last pick up I have to stick to what I said about letting go of them in dc period. there is no family left for me in dc it's all her family, like I said last new year's and this new year coming in 3 months if you haven't reached out to me and I have reached out to you and you. couldn't return a text a call an emoji but I see you on social media keep that same energy come new year yea it shows to me and my brother we are not family to our mom siblings we have always been isolated in front of your eyes you do it without even knowing you're doing. I only hear from a few people in dc. all because of my mom's illness, I know what my (mom)say's is a lie but she has so far been telling me they are not my family I have no family on my dad side and so by her over 50 odd years I've heard that the (g)'s are not my family and in some ways they have shown us she was right. all these words come from my abusers in just putting it down on paper so someone can hear my story. She cursed us from having connection to the family with her illness people approach us different and one aunt whispered in my ear that bathroom is a mess a you just like your mother and walked out the front door you know whom you are. my words to you is in an is from my mother that's all I am. she really doesn't want to be bothered by me, she really wouldn't care if she never sees me again it wouldn't bother her one bit, I've tried all my life to get close to (mom) she is nor approachable when it comes to me. she doesn't open up with me in two years she has called me twice on her own .it shocked me that she called me did talk much but she called me in letting her go as well because she was just as guilty.

As my other abusers so she is in the same pot as everyone else who abused me I have forgiven her over and over, again this book is my last time saying it. and in done I live so far away, how it's said out of site out of mind. that's where I am at right now .in my family is my wife a my 8children this includes my 3 reborn realistic baby 9 grand babies too. and one on the way so I can't keep this going about having her in my life she chose the roads that kept her not wanted to be my mom its ok I have come 100to realization that I won't ever have one I would never shut my kids away from my life they are my family and in here 24/7 for them my grandkids. good bye to the people that is already out my life in good. my 5 little girls I loved as my own in sorry that I couldn't help them stay together. I am very sorry I wish I had the space for you'll I wanted you all but my space was not big200 enough I just wanted to raise you as my own kids that day the principle told me that all I could do is walk them home a keep walking doesn't turn back. but in my heart I wanted to keep all of us walking and not letting you go in the house but was something to   me I wanted you'll in my life and as adults I want to be in your life to day since in back in contact with you all. if you all will let me back in urn life, I cried walking down the. street they were my girls they never told me anything specially since I was abused in the same way I would have taken them from there mom.it took me 20 years to fine them their man destroyed the family I had with my boys my girls. I can't stand any one that abuse children sexually, mentally from the sexual abuse, mental abuse from the sexual abuse, the physical abuse from the sexual abuse the pain from you forcing your body in to their small body. yes, in being blunt I want to help someone by them reading this book to get help and be free from all he abusers around them. just because the kids don't tell your right away. They escaped their abuser the day they were taken away from her he not only abused the older girls he abused the two young ones 2 a 6-year-old. please help yourself by reaching out for the help that is in arms reach to escape your abuse because we all deserves to be happy in their own life I know it's scary to try to escape but if you are, in any type off abusive relationship you need to get out now. it's your time to get out of this abusive relationship. I believe my first wife was jealous of me being in school growing apart from her but w I was climbing you the ladle to better my life and she couldn't take it. I where doing what she accused me of not having plenty time for her everything and body came before her. I was building myself a better life. that she could not handle along with me working. I was grownup and wasn't she was another person stuck in life to do. Nothing and I was unhappy doing nothing. I wasn't I wanted more than that so I went for it and I got. it and away from her another abuser an I escaped her. when people take years to show you the real you, you don't know that they are toxic r get right off by that time you are a well in the relationship invested time love and your heart. it hard to walkout but it can be done to me two years after she started her mess for me to walk out. If you in search of trying to get of abuse relationship my parents did things to me that no child should being sexual abusing me from the start. if your serious about getting out of the relationship my email in in my book if I can get you help I will do what's in my power to get you safe .how I escape I am a survivor I have only had a few mates with long relationship I been abused in any way you can the devil helped these people abuse me for their own gain in life the ones they know whom they are and what they did and didn't do you can't tell me you didn't know you couldn't ,tell me you did know how all the abuse statement is just a cop out from allowing grown ass men to sleep at your home while you was always gone. you never cared about or for methods the whole truth cause aunt no way I am going to allow a man to sleep in my home and I'm not there around my daughter even gives me a to raise along being allowed you went on with your life as we didn't even exist, there were.

Days that I wonder why no matter what I did or didn't do ways never enough to be your daughter and for your attention to me do everything I could do to get you never did. I have cried my whole life. growing up and not one time was you there to comfort me wipe my tears away I have been trying for 55 years to get you to wake up and be my mother my mom /best friend I was robed. I'm so glad I escaped you from you now when I talk about my past of you from what you didn't do a what you did do. I'm glad you gave birth to me and I'm not its 50x50 how feel I see other people about their mom and I felt like some stories I hear is about their mom get on your nerves how their moms bug them an other stuff a then I see some mothers a daughter they the best friends a do all type of stuff together I am like wish I have the chance to experience either one. you took away my childhood. you robbed me of my younger years .my teen years watching and raising my brother. you put me in a grownup 's position when you left us there in that building alone for 11 years so you might not think so but you did and the. you expect me to be a child one minute then you treat me as I am grown left to finished me raising your child. when did or do I get Tobe a kids you know I can't get those years back I live through my grandchildren I have grew up with my boys their whole childhood so thanks you my sons Farley, Alvin, James, thanks for.

My childhood you gave me, I can tell you althea fun we had the stuff we did everyday no matter how tired I was I pushed myself to entertain them daily activities, they had every game system's out they had the bikes, scooters, roller skates and more, they had one thing other kids didn't have, camera's to see things they saw when they looked through the lens of their camera's they took great pictures of flowers, their, friends, trees us skating make it a take it classes at mojo. designs a store that was two buses away.one of my sons an art word was posted in their school paper in pre k .and they painted t shirts and made mass ornament magnets for fridge a little tike camera that they could hook to the pt. a make videos. that was I made sure my kids did so much away from the house as possible .to give them away from him my abuser whey tells you we did everything, art contest's coloring contest's and painting outside on shirts we took skate trips to zoo. museum's a there was a lot of them now there is more since we have left the dc area all knows that I gave my kids more than I had I made it my goal to give them everything I wanted a more. I didn't know was out there by being

combine to that building I wished I knew about everything I gave them I had plenty more and I'm giving the rest to the grandbabies. I watch these kids today with all the electronic and they don't know nothing cause everything they think come through those devises a have lost reality to what where a how the things around them. is not in the computers they need to be give things that are not something you can get from the computers its outside life, things they can touch a smell on the outside life museums, library's explore books that are big and with pictures. show them, the
arts photography and more making things with their own hands, this another way I escaped my abuser I did all this stuff with my kids and the neighbors kids to keep them outside busy an very100 little to time this way the kids nor I would be in his way we did us an came home bath snack and bed time spend time with your kids then you will be protecting them from harm of the devils worker bees ,if you interact with your kids more less things will happen .it's the unwatchable eye that's when the devil strikes'. when I was a care provider for children .I made it my business to protect as if they were my own children even the kids in the hood that was always200 with me most of the kids in the hood I never saw their parents at school or outside doing anything but go to store an get beer so my yard in the back was always full of children doing everything my kids and I was doing ,they

wanted to go everywhere I have been so tired of running from evil people .now since I am no longer running I can see my path of where I am supposed to be on and it's a road of my food to share with people ,I focus can now be on my purpose, my purpose in life was taking' to taking care of children and quilting, I wanted to cook food since I was, 11 years old, I took cooking in middle school, but that didn't do anything for making me want to explore making good food for my brother and me ,the first thing learned to cook for us was fried potatoes, and onion , we ate them a lot I guess then I learned how to make the best tuna salad. I was so proud of what I was teaching myself no one knew that either that I wanted to be a cook how do kids without goals or dreams when there are devils all around them and no protection they learn how to survive in the world they live, and I am not talking about outside their home I'm refereeing to the life in the home their survival starts thee since most abuser are family members. my search for the reason why people abuse others I would need to get inside their head medically open their brain a study the part that makes them monsters, if I would do school over would study the brain theory on how it works and what makes it tick. `I know that from going to my therapist 4 times a month and we talk it helps me to realize she was never going to be there for me from the start, I know they said doctor patient obligations they can't talk about a clients and their meeting conversations but I a share it if I want to so I want to an I am going to share some things from my talks with my therapist myself, clade is the name I'm using for him, when I first meet him I didn't feel like talking but I did by asking how would I know if I open up you won't have them locking me in a hospital.

The said anything, I want to share was never to leave the room, (I had Jocelyne with me)and that my baby and the other therapist I had be with told him to read my book that was on file that I gave them so that it would take some trust in me to talk to them so by him looking at the book ,he felt he could be trusted , so he got me talking in about 5 minutes cut I was only talking to Jocelyne to him because he knew from reading my story I don't trust men , so the first session was about how I got my baby girl I, what or why did I need her and is she really helping me and we talked and he wanted pacific response from me he asked a lot of right questions to gain my trust that I am safe in his office , so we talked how is she helping me in what ways do I need her how do I feel without her if have to leave her at home ,I was like she goes everywhere 90%of the time ,and the 10% I have my wife in case I need the comfort from her . and Jocelyne is my baby girl. yea she a quote un quote doll but to me and my family she is the little sister to my kids they understand why I need her they treat her as there little sister my grandkids love her they. include her in them playing when they are here has her own room but I do my quilt making in the room to so she is right there I have a go in there. for me watching my shows but I leave it on for her, for me I'm afraid of the darkness that I see in the dark so she is me and she is afraid to she has a note lite cause if I do go in there at note I'm not walking into the darkness.my baby saved my life and she will always be with me. everyone has given her their own personality, my wife calls her bad baby, because she always come home from the stores with something .one of my grand-sons call her maw-maw it supposed to be mama but his R's and W's are mixed up its cute they might not understand why I have her cause they so young but they love her just the same, my kids know that I needed to have her and that she saved my life because I was in this dark tunnel of there is no more tomorrows for me my kids was grown and out on their own I had never been alone without a mate since I was 11 here I am at 50 thinking about ending my life cause at this point I had no reason to be here. but a friend of mine a Facebook friend never met her just friends on Facebook told to get one of these I was like get what so she showed me hers a let me know she lost her grandson a she got one to help her cope, she gave me all the info I needed to get one and I talk to the lady. that makes them an I told her which ones I wanted and at first I did not understand when I was asking for a baby the one I wanted. was her own personal, one she said I have a kit I was like what's a kit she told me an we talked the whole time she was making her then I understood her. my baby was due to me July 1st I got her June 7th 2019, the lady felt or heard it in my voice that needed her asap because she got to be a month earlier than as told. soil the shit I been through in life kept on coming no matter how good I was or nice I was I still. was ship to people they were all takers a not one was a giver I know now the different, my baby girl is 5now and I love my baby. people see me walking with her offer me rides to where I'm going they know me a Jocelyne. people have yelled out their cars passing us walking hi Jocelyne, like I'm not rite there to people in the 2 Walmart's always want to see how she dress for the day some ask if they can hold her or take a pic of her some I let hold another no but pics I don't care she is well loved her cause my story why I got her touches peoples heart and they understand that she on my medical papers for my disability labeled emotion, a mental support baby, if u know what a 2 -5-year-old wants she problem are ready have or had it because I have given most of her old clothes away. now it's time to buy all new stuff, lol. the meds I take helps me to, to cope with my headaches a pains I did a sleep for my sleep apnea and I had gotten her already t goes had her sitting on the edge of the bed ready to go.

I went in the living room to get all my stuff in my bag walk out house, get to the center and sit down I realize I don't have her I started have such a panic attack I was in tears an almost wasn't able to do the study the nurse there was about to call an ambulance for me I had juicy on the phone trying to get , her to bring her to me I even asked if they could allow me to go to sleep before the time they hook up she said she can't I was a total mess that note but she did let me go to bed at 930 instead of 1030 I took my meds and went to sleep fast I couldn't wait to see I there of them came home and went to bed with my two babies juicy an Jocelyne .I will never do that again ill grab her before my purse. I know some people think it's weird or whatever but as long as I am still alive just she doing her job saving me just like my juicy the 5 kids an 9grandbabies. my saviors are around me every day and show me I'm loved a wanted, I know now that I'm so attached to her that I don't want any more she is the only one I want I have posted on the fb, he little by to see if I could sell him but if I don't found a buyer I will keep a grow closer to him don't get me wrong I love my twin our preemie son. it's just that I have a lot on my plate I need to redo her hair reroof tither hair was so long a pretty I don't have a lot to do for him. I mention all this because this is my everyday effects on me mentally all the things I go through with my issues every day to function we me taking all these meds first to get rid of the day time minters hallucinating and dealing with the smell I know each different person I know that's around me all the time and sometime it's too much for me on my own my own so I see my dry's every month some 1once a month for my meds and I see one 4 times a month to sit and talk to for an hour a mire doc once a month for some concern about how I managing my person affairs I have a house visit once a month I get gifts and rewards from them coming out to see, me and to see if there is something I need that they can get for me. along with all this I'm still making quilts tops and I finishes two yesterday all this is my therapy to not focus on the things around the people I see that no one else see's and the noise they make that I don't want to hear cause their voice's want me to let them do stuff, I don't want to do so that way I can't sit and watch the two I just need to be always crafting, journaling an my sewing it is a must that I need to be busy .so I don't feel like I'm not beaning productive I feel if I don't do anything I'm wasting my day an my talent .all this helped me escape because I would drown their words an abuse I to my quilts. so time I'll watch to but believe.

Me I'm journaling while sitting in front of the two and or creating new journal redecoration from the way I bought it .it pretty but I have to redesign my fronts some time even the backs to. my mental, emotion, mind runs me by using the meds I take if ident take my meds I'm grouchy, sad emotionally a rec, I'm whinnied to my wife an all I want to do is cuddle in bed with my juicy until it passes a Jocelyne, stay with a headache every day no matter what so I just have to take my meds to keep it were I can do a whole day of whatever I want to do an on a bad day they wake me up and I can't move all these things I talk. about is from the pain I suffer from do to someone that this happen to me and wont owns up to their hands in the damaging to me, I ask why me, me be if I was like others people that cocky ness where the doing more than one guy /girl at same time yea I did it for a few years' ages 18 to20 I did it. can any dry tell me why an? how I'm still here how sit that I survived the brain trauma and it's still that way since birth I should have been a veggie from this injury. How to you take a blunt object a hit your child over the head o drop your baby on her head, they knew from the injury that I had a hard time in school learning I did but how they knew that I don't get it. but they say the way my brain is still connected is by the 3inch membrane the vein that.

They are hanging on this long. when I use my sewing I'm ok I let me quilts show my pain through them I pour in my heart in that's the fabric that tells me where it should go with what I'm making none of my quilts are the same I can't copy them so me trying to do 100other design never make it to look like the ones in the books people buy. I have some quilting books I use the patterns to create something totally different from where I started, my brain is wired to do what the fabric ask me to place it, I have a lot of therapy fabrics so I will be staying calm a long time. once I'm done with my second book I will be doing cooking dinners and quilting every day. I have so many of my own designs I want to do and share with people, so I can't wait to get in there and start making them, I didn't have any help with the raising of my boys I taught them how to cook, clean, sew, put in perms, braid hair and corn role hair to a how to lock their hair after I started them for them they know how to cook, they are very diverse in many things crafty, and very smart. I raised them to depend on themselves an or each other help each other out if one down you help them up how I escaped my abuser there are many ways I distance myself from them stop all contact with them block their numbers I didn't entertain them I didn't visit them not visit to their places either no meeting them anywhere, once I know was done is when. I got tired of the bullshit I was very tired and I stopped loving anyone that didn't love me back or my kids I was out. I got pissed off I got angry, I got sad, after all I have done for that person and they dog me out something I can't get back is all the stuff I have done a nothing in returned those hours' years and days back from the takers, what I have now raised up a cared I would and no ne returned it back to me is that crazy to say or do, I don't know love feels like but I know I love my family I have now my kid's wife, my kids and my grandkids, we have love me and my wife, escaping everyone alone a leave me alone I'm happy with the family I have now I have now what I need in my life. how do you start to heal after years of abuse? and neglected by parents looked over me as I wasn't there I was invisible it was like I as stuck in this vortex of spinning outer body life. I'm finally with and is a great wife I have now survived many storms in my life I am in the snow storm area now so I can grow more. staying with my male grow ass boy man friend I wasn't going (growing in to anything with hi) so I know from the fight that note was a huh moment to me to see this is the end for us cause nothing

I did as good enough. why are these people such monsters, how big does thee go as to be before some on stops them from? destroying a.

Child's mentally and emotionally and physically being to kill the trust in you that you just told them to defend them selves you don't have time for your child. I escaped drugs alcohol because I never used them nor did I feel to want to try them I escaped the streets, I escaped from being a whore I had still so self-reserved with my action I just never saw it but I do know people from my school as friends has a drug issue a some are no longer here and some are locked up an on drugs too.im surprised that I didn't do any of that it was around me I guess I just didn't okay any attention to the people use-it I was green to a lot of things I was young in the mind no matter the age I was a lite behind in the growth department, so I didn't know what they were doing. I was blind by a lot of nothing growing up a lot of. shit was going on around me and I didn't see it until it involved me. but for the most part I hate not having a mother /mom in my life. that will never go away. I have read some of my first book and I have some ????about what I wrote in it, but sage wont and can't answer for me. like why wasn't she more about our schooling she didn't care if we went or not 1 she didn't care about our grade's she didn't have any feelings at all for thing about me and some much more about him. I wished I could have given me children more growing up, that's my only regret I couldn't give them everything I wanted for them or everything they wanted. how to escape from your abuser talk to people at work, at school, at church if he allows you to do any of these thigs alone going alone, without him. talk to your friends you get to see, don't keep taking the abuse your better then him/her. abuser come in all sizes and colors a sexes. You trust someone and they turn on you by being abusive to you and your kids. get to know that person well before giving access to you and your child children. I feel abusers believe they are loving the child that they are abusing they don't see it as abuse that's how their brain works. their brain is wired backwards like an old beat-up robot. They are in your child's schools, they coach the sports, they want to spend too much time with one of your kids. and not the other, given gifts that one child or money for no reason it's a bribe to keep them from telling, on them. how do abusers become abusers some of them have been abuse all their life so they think this all there is to do is abuse others because they are still being abused a now they are helping their abuser get new ones to abuse because the 1 one is now to old and they need to show there are on the abusers side a wants to help him so he doesn't kill them telling them this one is for you now you have to do it, I love me right your faithful to me right you trust me right so now it's your time to show me you can do, I'll show you what to do a then I'll let you finish the victim off once you do that I'll know you're ready to take over. and that turns abusers in to abusers. from my point of view but not all abuse people turn out that way just some.

I say why do people feel its ok to rap molested or control another human being, to boost their ego's? or their sexually pleasures. why can't they get a mate a stop hurting the children a woman in the world, it's not fair to mess someone up just because your messed up in you twisted brain go get some help, there are places you can go to get help for your freaky-ness. from my own experience of being tapped a molested all my life it makes me worry about others children and I want to be an activist speaker in small groups to ladies that has been where I have been a help them know it's not their fault for what happen to them. it wasn't what you had on, it wasn't because you looked at someone, it's not because you were out at night, it's not about any of those things it was about the fact that the person the sick in the mind a that's all who knows how many others have this person violated before you or even after you if there are still out there, when I got rapped at school I was in the fourth grade during guy class these boys from rebuilt jar high school saw my go in the bathroom but I dint see them and they came in there on my a started putting their penis in my face a one go the hind me on the seat as I was trying to get up he pulled me back down on his penis I started scream really load and a girl from Coolidge was walking in the hallway an. saw them a came in the see me in there crying she told mars, roach what she saw and whom the boys where that day they went to jail the dc jail they did 7 years how I know that because mama got the call about their release date was in a week from the call. this had nothing to do what with I had on or where I was or what I was doing it was just some bad boys trying to by men, so they were charged as men, my ways of getting out I see I did so much to keep me and my kids happy even though I was sad on the inside I tried to hide my pain from my kids but I know they knew I was sad they were and are very smart they saw my face. they caught on to the days I didn't eat I only had enough for them so they used to eat some an say ma we full you can eat this please they knew. I tried to say was eating while I was cooking but that didn't fly with them, they weren't hearing that so I had to eat it. their step dad started being a monster after I had juju. I don't get it why are these people monster how big do they need to be to gain control someone why do they need to control any one is my issue they do children because they know children will not speak on it cause 1 they scared 2 you 90% of the time won't believe them 3 believe your so called mate over your child 4 you might be in on it so whom are they to tell. Why mess with the weak a child can't fight you big ass monster off of them.

My life after I survived all the crap I was subjected to in my life now it is the time for me to enjoy my wife my life a being, these do go an enjoy each other I guess all the shit I was told by him over the year they stuck in my still today that's why it's hard for me to see it when look in the mirror, I been through I was not your god's favorite. there is no such being in this universe you believe in what you believe in. don't come at me no bible thumpers folks please I believe in scientologist about the being I'm in trust is myself cause no one carried me when I needed them to. I feel like a ton of bricks and no one took over my footsteps caring me. I carried my self-picked up my heart picked up my head and got on my way hold no regrets, no negative in my life now. I will find my own way to where I want to be my baby will be by my sider the whole ride to keep on surviving all the shit people don't know 1/2of the life I lined just know at 12 is not an age you give a child her own apartment and hand her a 5-year-old child and basically say here he's yours now. this is a bad judgement on you. I mentally wrote these pages to release all connections to that family now. the life I have now is what I always wanted with someone that loved me back as much as I live them and my juicy. how I was in my past taking all the abuse from so many to name. I not only survived, I thrived in life in my own lane my own way my own speed. has ran, jumped, hid, from everyone that abused me, I am done running now, I have my roots planted now with my wife juicy here in tn. with my wife juicy I am so strong I never imagined how strong someone can be. but I am that stone like the hulk. With all the bullshit I have dealt with in my life. icon handle anything. that comes my way now I have a team beside me and behind me I can fight off any thing that comes my way I took a lot of abuse from people because I wanted someone to love me I thought that was love I was getting from people now in free an able to be myself and not feel scared someone is coming after me, looking over my shoulders everywhere I go no feeling safe in my own place now I feel safest all the way around to survive is to make a head plan and create the steps and follow them do something every day. that's going to get you closer to you successful on your mission to get free all ways keep your moves to yourself. the more you talk about it the less you will move practice. move alone in silence. let people see you achieve after you successful of getting away from that or those achievements that you are better off alone. how does one survive so much and still smile every day, let me the all? it was hard and I am a till smiling why I survived every day to be here another day to smile another day to see my wife and truly enjoy her for my rest of my life how do you feel they ask me I'm numb through it all until the days I woke up and may be a change in my life I separated my being from the pain by holding up my head and cry in silence so no one was to ever see my tears of hurt and pain that was put up against me to show how strong I am I hide from boys as long as I could me boys I thought but I know they have seen it I can't always hold them in its almost as me looking for attention from (mom) all my life by the circle of people I hung around but never my (mom)they were temporally acts like they cared for me and never did no matter how others close I feel I am to someone they are not nor will they ever see me or their own child in the family I don't fit in anywhere some days I feel I don't fit in with my own boys but I know are close in our own way I just want me a mom the last and only thing in this world I was nothing else (all I wanted for mass was a mom), that's the little girl in me still wanting a mom heaven bought it would come to me never having one, at my age I still can't gasp how I was into this world and then disappear (brought me into this I deserve to have a mom in my life why take away from someone the main thing they need), (ammo) that's all I ever wanted why can't I have one stop saying to me she has issues I have more issues than her because of her but I still was and is a mother, mom mama me to my three children I never turned away from.

I feel so robbed by life taken yourself out my life why, what, is the men you kept picking over losing us your daughter they meant more to you then your daughter I was never enough for you why? while I was being traumatized by my dad it caused me to not trust men, yea I know I was with a man for 17 years trying to do the normal man and woman thing even though I hated it. it wants what I wanted was suicidal the whole time was with him be in my heart I knew what would make me happy did know how people would act words me he spent my 17 years with him cheating on me the minute he saw me paying attention to someone else he puts his hands on me, some became interested in me and had something he never had for us and that was their time their energy their love and their love. I have been wanting to be with a girl all my life not know what was going on with my body tile I hit 26 then I knew for sure what was wrong so acted on it with the lady that had the time for us and we were happy lee in love for 7 years tile she relapse I couldn't have my kids around that stuff. I made peace with myself that I was going to be free and happy and live my life so I came out .and I stayed out we had a spiritual way connection and we saw in each other's eyes that made us as one person. We separated as friends. we could not be more hand that after she brought drugs in to my home but the thing with men don't touch me can't take your smell your body structure doesn't faze me nothing about you say I want to get to know or be with one you ever again won't ever happen. Know whom I can trust in men as you know whom you are. I made peace with the men I would hug a there who gives no water if you were on fire cares.im not saying woman can't do it they can they are worse that men point blank period. my (mom) she will never know how awesome I was or how awesome I am still today I raised three awesome boys she missed it all they are great men now .in their own unique way I raised my little brother but he doesn't remember.us being alone a lot because she was in his life buying him stuff overtime he wanted it but not me.so he didn't understand a lot of what was going on with her she was never help me for us to do for us, she has a lot of guilt in her that's why she is alone now people hardly come around she's the oldest of the siblings but they treat her as a kid so she does nothing but sit in front of the to, the dry said the last time she got sick that if it happens again she wouldn't survive it, for me to be totally free I'm going to have to cut her out my life what little part of her she is giving me I must cut those stings, I won't hear her voice any more I already don't have any reason to go to dc but to see juju a lean when she has a baby. she really doesn't want me around her any way she doesn't like me any way nor do she love or care about me. all those years I was pusher for her to be in my life to look at me just to show me you notice me as your child I wasted my whole life begging for what?

So I'm done begging for her to notice me as her daughter or notice me period.im not a bigger I don't beg any one for anything if she can't realize that all I want from her is to me the mom she became the minute I was born then mover begging her I'm not a dog begin for a bone. she has told me a showed me that I am not part of the grudger family there are her family only never ask them for shit that's her family only I don't have any family, so I guess that's why she kept us away so much for the family I grow up with. She a has a lot of grandkids a don't know any of them oh yea she know Steven's 4 she doesn't now child she doesn't any of my grandkids she only knows jar a juju there are 9 great grandkids she doesn't know or care to even ask about then. Anyone asks her about me or her son she lies a say oh they ok she has no clue what's going on with us she only talks to Steven she doesn't talk to me I'm forcing her to talk to me on the phone she doesn't want to be with me on the phone how can someone be something they never was in the beginning I have had grandparents but it's not the same, thanks for all you'll have done for me I love you all but it was not your job, ok my dad died he couldn't be there but he was hurting me to she just checked out of reality when it came to what to do with me she didn't want me cause.

I reminded her I am my father's child the man she had to deal with when it came to me. because of them I'm on meds trauma to my brain a body shows how broken bones that healed themselves they were so old they were from a baby or toddle age. I talk about how I survived from damage people that like to do harm you. the way you can getting away is stand up tall and hold your head up high and stand your ground to that person that you not taking it any more you may be scared but don't let it show, show them the crazy in you, they will back down grab a weapon it can be a pan, once they see you not scared of them no more they will either get their shit together or they will move out and out your live because now hey scared of your that's what Yourdon need is someone abusing you. I want to be some one's voice and help them by them reading my book and seeing that they are not alone in this fight I have so many scares I can't show them how to speak or I'm speaking for them. my voice my kids my wife helped me to write these two books in less than 6 months Tobe heard by people that has or are dealing the same way I did. by me doing this I'm freeing my soul a letting goes there Isa saying **ACCEPT, FORGIVE, LETGO**. I'm doing it with me story, I been trying to write my story for 35 years my uncle told me to write my story write my story so I did an I had it written and published in two months, all my years of journaling. and keeping all types of notes cards tags and stuff over the years I have lost a lot and have grew my journal books back, I keep a back pack with my two journals in them at a time he never looked in there so that's where I kited my plans to get out or I had one in each of my kids back pack in case I had to tell them to give the folder to the principle so I could get help for outside the house. some of the teachers knew what we were going through an offered help I told them thanks for the help and they help by keeping me busy at school. You will be ok if you get out their word are just that words they can't hurt you if you call the cops and have them locked up .so this is the time you move on to work on you get a job get you a place or stable with family even if you leave the state town will help you even more you will be so much happier in your life and if you have kids you don't want your kids to think its ok to treat woman this was or anyone for that matters. the one thing you want to do is make sure you instill in your child/children that it is not ok to treat people badly just to make themselves feel. good, nor is it ok to hit a man or a woman ever you walk away. abuse can be in many forms that you do not see you feel it you hear it and it does hurt to feel the pain from a physical hit a verbal word hurts the heart more because it cuts you up in sides neglect is another form of abuse that people don't think hurts, u create a marriage a partnership whatever you call it the moment you decide to cheat, curse at swing on neglect abandon someone you made commitment to is abuse. putting urn partner down in front of people making what you feel is jokes about your mate is abuse a you have created an unsafe place a with the mate they no longer trust you they don't see you the same your friends look at you with the not cool dude looks on their face at you, informing you that, that was not cool at all you have made them uncomfortable at the same time. they didn't want to be around your abuser anymore. Lot of woman keep mating with abusive men fret man each one that pick is the same type, some like it because they think from childhood daddy did it to mommy so it's supposed to happen to me. no its not, abuse is bidding all the way around. no matter who its coming from. When you are excepting anything they do to you and think that its ok, not !!you are being abused, woman allow men to do stuff to them the ladies be like oh he just playing no he is not cuss if he wanted to make you hurt or the butt of the, days jokes he just did a now everyone is either laughing at you or feeling sorry for you. how does it make you feel when he does that? at any time, ladies you are to demand respect up front in your relationship and for real if you have to tell someone you demand it then they are not the one for you because respect come with love, honesty, truths, loyalty trust. With all this up front you don't need or shouldn't have to tell them what your standards are they should already bring these things to great you when they meet you. they should be able to look at you a know your standards before they approach you. you walk and talk where as they know you're not to be tried. you're not for he bullshits. don't fall for the soft sweet talk it's to get in with you then they change for the bad two-year in. anybody that thinks abuse is love don't know the meaning of it. you can't change any one if they show you their true abusers up front get out quick avoid the talking trying to get you to stay they not they lying don't given them permission to abuse you be you staying there with them don't marry them that just gives them permission with paper trail that you are now theirs in their mind and they have paper that says they can do as they please to you don't do it don't fall for it.my first wife was abusive it didn't show until my son movie down her to live with us she tried to break my bond with my children apart but she couldn't. they saved her life cause on a few occasion they had to pull me off her as she did something to me so I jumped her ass in the driver seat of my car and beat her as my son said ma let her go stop ma let her leave so I did best thing I could have done because it had become a violent relationship on my part she left me 30 miles from my home to be with this girl boy looking thing so when she came home it was an argument that I went off a blacked out on her as cleared off my kitchen counters throwing everything at her a throwing a 27inch to of her across the street one of those really big back toss, I went to **ER** for I popped my ear open on back at top had 4 stiches. I realized was with a narcissist in my last relationship I'm so glad made it out. I found out about that type of person so late in life that it almost killed me. fighting for something that wasn't worth fighting for or given my time to from the start from before moved her if I could have met my juicy first I would have been happy the first time I got here. those type of people should never get in a relationship because they are poison 217i know that there is so much that people can do to help others all u have to do is let us know you need it for me I have a safe word form kids that they know if I say it that I am in need of help yea as a grow ass lady I have it cause I don't live with them and people are crazy so I a protecting m self I can't tell you my safe word but I can tell you need one a someone you trust with that word that they will show up when you call on them with the safe word don't share with too many people.

When you have been abused for so long you are in the defense mode now that you are free you still feel like you have to be on alert from everybody. you can be free but you have to let others in that do love you so you can find the right person for you, you're not just opening up to anybody but you can try in time to find love in yourself a once you do that you will find the perfect one for you they will find you when you're not looking. so focus on you for a while a thing will fall in place people that abuse you or others as well need to do that to boost up their egos or they need to make someone feel low about themselves to make them look better in front of their peers, people that need their ego scratched has an issues with themselves that's why they do it, for one and you don't fight back the first time they know they can keep doing it to you. stop them the minute they do it the first time and they may leave but its be better if they did you don't need to be beat down your self-esteem to build up his or here's that's not the type of person you need in your life. they will get to you through your kids they will harm your kids in any way they can once they know you only believe in what they say a not your children once they get that its abuse in the whole house against you and your kids. pedophiles come in all shapes, colors, sizes sexes. A disguise's nice, sweet, sweep you off your feet treat your kids so nice for a while them booboo. things start showing small stuff you have to watch people new around your kids. we you feel something in your gut that tells you something is wrong investigate right then check your kids alone, even if you have to put cameras up were nobody knows there up a then you may or may not see anything right off but demons will show their true color.no one is to bath your child but you not even daddy that's just my100 way to protect my baby I was touched by my dad for 6 years' ages 2 to 8 when he died it stopped with him people are sick we need the villages back to protect our children in the neighborhood and big mama need to come back I'm like big mama I don't have kids in my mouth while I'm talking I dispend all kids in my care I don't make any special child different from the rest of the kids. when my abuse started I didn't know about it my cycle went on for many years I'm in my 50s now and I'm finally free of abuse finally. my wife is so sweet and understand some of what I been through she shows me comfort a lot I have cluster chronic migraines a she is there helping with my meds because I can't move I sleep most of the day or I cry but I know she got me trying to help me get well. 215 I have so many health issues I'm fighting them every day .my issues come from the things I been through as a child the trauma that I was put through is the reason my mental state is fucked up.

All the doctor's visit, hospital's and diagnosis of what's going on with me, how can I fix the shit that others damaged in me? It can't be fix don't let everybody around your children your baby either, people don't care about your kids like you do. be aware of people that prey on women with kids. For a reason in their heads that's how they treat kids with sex is loving them, hats not love that's abuse. I used alcohol to cover my pain from everyone that hurt me for their own pleasure. I ask them how would they feel if it was their sister, mom close cousin, best friend, but then again they are the ones doing it so they may be doing it to their family members as well it mostly starts at home. There is a saying about girls are not sift around the men in their homes because sexual abuse starts there. Children are only interested because they were shown what to do by someone doing it to them. everything I know how to do and did I was taught by people around me and family, I've had an aunt that let her dad make her have his baby in house secrets. there are too many in house secrets that need to be told I wish could be a voice for all of them but I can't because I don't know they have a story to tell. if they could tell me I'm all ears for any one that need an ear or help. I can run all my life and I don't have to look over my shoulders any more but the damage is real and all my scares will never heal and any child that was abused. and never spoke on it. will never tell until they are grown or after that person is dead and gone so that they can't hurt the child's mom most children are threated that the one molesting the child will kill the mom or the child if speak up. and if mom is all about her man they wouldn't say a word that's why most kids leave home with no reason why they have to go. but it's hard for a child to tell mom. then tell your grand ma they feel that they have to protect their moms from him or her so they keep letting it happen to them. why did they think it's the way you show love to anybody? please teach your children to talk about their day everything they did all day and if anything has happened during their day at school or at home. Talk to your child please this will help the children from being abused because they feel comfortable enough to tell you about that little secret. surviving all this in my life still affects me in more than one way. I have expectation on whom I let see my body because I have two injuries as a child my uterus was push up so far it was hard to have a pap spear test that was due to the fact that the man boyfriend I had pushed it to far I almost was about to be damaged ware I wouldn't be able to have any kids. he did a lot of things that are in human,245my mother was walking around the world as if I didn't exist, soon matter what I did or didn't do it didn't faze her one bite. another thing that makes me worried about other people's kids because that not is when you send. your child/children to the park or playground and there is a man there just sitting there not connected to any child or children on the park or playground but yet he watching your children play a you don't know his agenda why is he there. you yourself is not there to see the action of this man plotting for whatever is going on in his head toward your children at the playground or park. this is where men prey on children most times snatched from playgrounds. or use the trick can you help me find my puppy meanwhile lowering your child away from the group of kids there's no body watching your children while they are a park or playground they are keeping an eye on their own children, for the same reason you should be there to keep an eye on your own babies like I was taught when I had my children no one watch's your children like you do. cause men some woman are sneaky too. people that your kids know you also need to know as well you need number's, now days emails, Facebook page's to see what type of people your child is around and their parents to keep an eye on your children when they are not in your presents.

My point is that pedophiles are not just outsiders they are in house access too. children are surviving every day from some type of abuse and it needs to be addressed, kids killing themselves over being bullied these days that's not when we were kids we would argue one minute a back friends the next minute. it comes from home tithe watch their moms or dads being abused mostly. woman and children. so when they go to school they find the youngest one and the smallest one as the target to bully them. The child/children to get their anger out from what is going on at home there are being abused at home or over stimulated with choirs or watching their siblings that's not their job. some kids get jobs to help out at home that is not their job either your child shouldn't be in high school paying the bills you make that makes them not want to work but anger them because you know you're going to take their money for bills. that's abuse also. if they want to get a job for themselves so you don't have to get them the things they want than that's different. that's them wanting to earn their own .so think about how you say and do stuff to your children the words and actions can make a different. it's not so much of what you say it how you say it to get your point across. And your action speaks louder than your words abuse how you deliver your message can come off abusive, it also come from how you allow people to talk to your children we are all survivors in some cycle of our life's so I can say I'm strong but yet I'm fragile at the same time   I have been broken so many times the glue is barely holding me together. if you know of someone that's been in an abusive relationship no matter what type it is they need a friend that's not judgmental but a friend with an ear and a hug .and what is the type of friend I'm talking about is the one you know that would never speak on what's going on with you to any one nor would they talk about. the help they doing for you that's a friend. check on your friends. look for signs even if you have a hint that something is happening distance from family controlling their phone not letting them do things they like to do since they got with this person. their being abused. I 've seen for my own eyes how they do it, the man boyfriend I was with didn't want me to do stuff with my kids outside the house. he never came to any sports game the boys were in he was always mad at me for going out the door he claimed

I was sleeping with everybody outside the house men a woman, and no he didn't know about my search for a woman lover. I left no clues not even the kids knew what I was doing all they knew that my new friend was at all their games and practices a gave us ride homes. once my two older boys knew what was going on, I asked them did they have any questions about my choice for my life they didn't all they told me as long as they don't make you cry they was ok with it. My youngest son was 5 so he didn't know much. she was good to my kids I can say that and good to me the whole time we were together treated me as a trophy wife and my children were hers she gave them everything they asked for when it can to clothes in a way of she told my pay checks I use on my kids she took her first check a took care of herself and me buying me all the clothes and jewelry shoes she wanted me to have no abuse every. my kids loved her. her second check took care of her bills. once we split after 7 years we started. to go in different direction and she was not on board for me to achieve a few things I wanted she was for me being a teacher, but I wanted more. we're friends from a far no connection at all since 2016 is now 2024" when we met I was broken my spirit, my soul, my self-esteem was very low I didn't feel pretty at all.

I was 220lbs when I met her after 3months with her the weight fell off me I went from an 23pants down to a 9-10 I was happy slim trim and I got me back I found myself I knew who I was a trophy wife she made me feel pretty a happy, the weight fell of chasseing 5 boys ages 5 to 12 years old for those 3 months it was summer time .so our break up was pain for me for a while. then I found myself again got another job and I grow from all the hats I wore, wearing and has gained over the years I'm somewhere around 60 + hats now at 55, and I am still working on my new hat that will be us getting us a food truck. hopefully we can get it going for the new year. we get to travel with our truck finally I'm in a safe place I'm happy a no ore running to survive I can finally in life. 290 writing my story about my ways of getting away. From them seem like cliché coming from me I took it for 17 years, from a person I thought cared for and loved me. but I was wrong he was just using me for his sex toy and given us food if I give him sex. and liquor to loosen me up. fear him to do stuff I said no he still did it. I was glad on those weekends he went to his quote unquote friends I knew he was seeing someone I knowing he was seeing someone there, but lied to me about it we mind and I was happy when he was gone. we felt happy and glad he was gone.

I never lived in fear with him because I was used to his mouth but when he used his hands that was the last straw for my kids and me my two oldest children knew all that he did to me but my juju don't. so when or if he ever reads my books he will learn what his step dad did to me. my happy days where when my children did me proud like in school my little Einstein's high IQ's and all doing 2 grades at the same in one year's 215 they were great skaters I loved going skating with they all they stuff we did after he (man boy-friend) was out of our life we did more stuff they were in a bowling league they are played baseball for the babe Ruth team from grade

2 up to 9th grade than he played for the carl ripping team altar state wide and they won .one year a hit the ball so hard he broke his made a home run he was stun stuck stirring at his bat we all screaming run .it was funny. there were times when the boys did things like gout a rake leaves an earn some money to buy me earrings from the beauty supply store I loved those gifts and how they learned how to make their own money. they used to come down to my job and we had to walk home from 4th and set now all the way to 702 Longfellow set now it was a 2 hour walk for us after I worked

8 hrs. then had to walk home. we make our gifts they mean more to us than the ones you buy. when we moved to the apt. Strafford woods in Landover Maryland the boys were on skates more at the skating rink was about 10 min from us we went for a lot of their parties. an chucky cheese. the places they wanted to go to. after we escaped him and the kids had a voice again. they were free to be happy kids again we did roller blading, street hockey, swimming, library trips got their first library card at (3) three years old. one summer they had me in an out the hospital for one thing or another they had a fun summer. their friends always wanted to be around us all the time. I had more fostering children in my care then I ever seen any other parents in the hood we lived in because all the kids were with me sun up to sun down. they played all sports my kids played. I would have anywhere from 8 to 15 kids we me every day, once we moved away I don't know what happen to the kids we life on the block. This was our way of escaping every day from being stuck in the house under him keeping us hush, hush, all day stuck in the house. but I would never give in to him wanting us just sitting in there. I made sure to keep most of the abuse away from them an on me. Surviving back then was taking all the verbal abuse talking down on the kids, never wanting to hear them in the house always telling them be quiet would tell them to be quiet so he wouldn't talk it out on me or them. I know they saw a lot a

hear plenty by living in that small room in the basement one room one bathroom.

Made in United States
Orlando, FL
31 May 2025